WORD BY WORD BASIC

Second Edition

PICTURE DICTIONARY

Steven J. Molinsky • Bill Bliss

Contributing Authors
Dorothy Almanza
Deborah L. Schaffer
Carol H. Van Duzer

Illustrated by
Richard E. Hill

PEARSON
Longman

Dedicated to Janet Johnston in honor of her wonderful contribution
to the development of our textbooks over three decades.

Steven J. Molinsky
Bill Bliss

Word by Word Basic Literacy Workbook, second edition

Pearson Education, 10 Bank Street, White Plains, NY 10606

Editorial director: Pam Fishman
Vice president, director of design and production: Rhea Banker
Director of electronic production: Aliza Greenblatt
Director of manufacturing: Patrice Fraccio
Senior manufacturing manager: Edith Pullman
Marketing director: Oliva Fernandez
Production editor: Diane Cipollone
Assistant editor: Katherine Keyes
Associate paging manager: Paula Williams
Text design: Wendy Wolf
Cover design: Tracey Munz Cataldo, Warren Fischbach
Realia creation: Paula Williams
Illustrations: Richard E. Hill

ISBN 0-13-148232-7
ISBN 978-0-13-148232-6
Pearson Longman on the Web
PearsonLongman.com offers online resources for teachers and students. Access our
Companion Websites, our online catalog, and our local offices around the world.

Visit us at pearsonlongman.com.

Printed in the United States of America
1 2 3 4 5 6 7 8 9 10 – CRK – 12 11 10 09

CONTENTS

A CIRCLE THE SAME WORD

1. NAME	STREET	NUMBER	(NAME)	STATE
2. CITY	STATE	ADDRESS	CITY	LAST
3. STATE	STREET	FIRST	LAST	STATE
4. STREET	FIRST	STATE	STREET	LAST
5. ADDRESS	ADDRESS	NAME	NUMBER	CITY

B MATCHING

1. STATE   GARDEN STREET

2. ZIP CODE   227-93-6185

3. STREET   GLORIA SANCHEZ

4. TELEPHONE NUMBER   CA

5. NAME   323-524-3278

6. SOCIAL SECURITY NUMBER   90036

C FILL OUT THE FORM

NAME: _____
        FIRST   LAST

ADDRESS: _____
        NUMBER   STREET   APT.

         _____
        CITY   STATE   ZIP CODE

TELEPHONE NUMBER: _____

SOCIAL SECURITY NUMBER: _____

D FILL OUT THE FORM

NAME
    FIRST   LAST

ADDRESS
    NUMBER   STREET   APT.

    CITY   STATE   ZIP CODE

TELEPHONE NUMBER

SOCIAL SECURITY NUMBER

S T U V W X Y Z 0 1 2 3 4 5 6 7 8 9

E INTERVIEW

Talk to three people. Write the information.

Name   Telephone Number

1. _____   _____

2. _____   _____

3. _____   _____

F LISTENING

Listen and circle the words you hear.

1. (name)
   address

2. zip code
   apartment number

3. telephone
   social security

4. state
   street

5. middle
   city

6. first
   last

G JOURNAL

My first name is _____.

My last name is _____.

My address is _____.

My telephone number is _____.

A WHO ARE THEY?

1. grandmother   <u>b</u>

2. father   ___

3. son   ___

4. daughter   ___

5. mother   ___

6. grandfather   ___

B MATCHING

1. FATHER   sister

2. SISTER   mother

3. BROTHER   daughter

4. MOTHER   father

5. SON   brother

6. DAUGHTER   son

Aa Bb Cc Dd Ee Ff Gg Hh Ii Jj Kk Ll Mm

1. w <u>i</u> fe

   s _ ster

2. fathe _

   mothe _

3. hu _ band

   _ on

4. grands _ n

   br _ ther

5. b _ by

   d _ ughter

6. grandmo _ _ er

   grandfa _ _ er

brother	father	mother	son
daughter	husband	sister	wife

Parents

Children

1. <u>f a t h e r</u>

2. <u>m</u> _ _ _ _ _

3. <u>h</u> _ _ _ _ _ _

4. <u>w</u> _ _ _

5. <u>s</u> _ _

6. <u>d</u> _ _ _ _ _ _ _

7. <u>b</u> _ _ _ _ _ _

8. <u>s</u> _ _ _ _ _

Nn Oo Pp Qq Rr Ss Tt Uu Vv Ww Xx Yy Zz

A WHO ARE THEY?

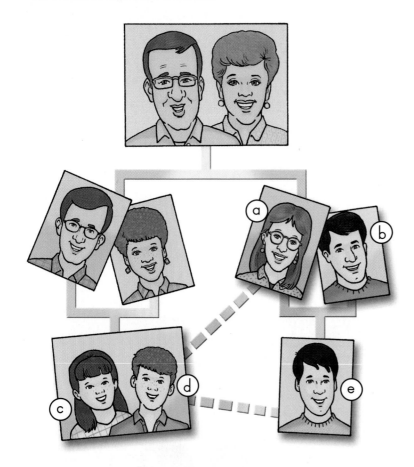

1. nephew   d

2. aunt   ___

3. niece   ___

4. cousin   ___

5. uncle   ___

B WHAT'S MISSING?

1. a u n t

   _ n c l e

2. _ e p h e w

   _ i e c e

3. c o u s i _

   u _ c l e

4. _ o n – i n – l a w

   _ i s t e r – i n – l a w

5. m o _ _ e r – i n – l a w

   f a _ _ e r – i n – l a w

6. s i s t _ _ – i n – l a w

   b _ o t h _ _ – i n – l a w

| aunt | cousin | nephew | niece | uncle |

n e p h e w   c _ _ _ _ _ _   a _ _ _

u _ _ _ _ _   n _ _ _ _ _

D **WHO ARE THEY?**

| aunt | uncle |

1. He's my _____uncle_____.

2. She's my _____.

| father | aunt |

5. He's my _____.

6. She's my _____.

| nephew | niece |

3. He's my _____.

4. She's my _____.

| sister | uncle |

7. He's my _____.

8. She's my _____.

E **JOURNAL**

This is my family.

My _____'s name is _____.

My _____'s name is _____.

My _____'s name is _____.

A MATCHING

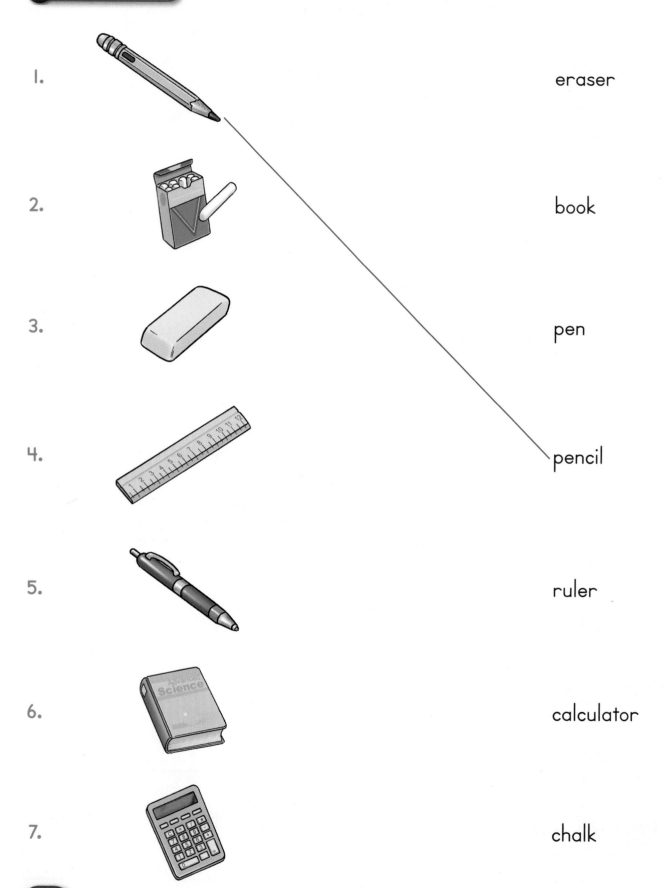

1.

2.

3.

4.

5.

6.

7.

eraser

book

pen

pencil

ruler

calculator

chalk

book	eraser	notebook	printer
calculator	marker	pen	ruler
chalk	mouse	pencil	workbook

1. p e n

2. _ _ _ _ _ _ _

3. _ _ _ _ _ _

4. _ _ _ _

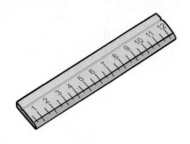

5. _ _ _ _ _

6. _ _ _ _ _ _ _ _

7. _ _ _ _ _ _

8. _ _ _ _ _ _ _

9. _ _ _ _ _

10. _ _ _ _ _

11. _ _ _ _ _ _ _ _

12. _ _ _ _ _ _ _ _ _

A WHAT'S THE WORD?

| board | bookcase | desk | map | | pencil | student |
| book | clock | globe | notebook | ruler | teacher |

a. _____map_____

b. _____

c. _____

d. _____

e. _____

f. _____

g. _____

h. _____

i. _____

j. _____

k. _____

l. _____

Listen and circle the word you hear.

1. pen   (pencil)

2. pencil   paper

3. chalk   clock

4. eraser   ruler

5. notebook   textbook

6. computer   calculator

C **WHAT'S IN THE CLASSROOM?**

Look at page 10 of the dictionary. Write the correct word.

| book | computer | globe | map | wastebasket |

1. There's a g l o b e on the bookcase.

2. There's a m _ _ next to the board.

3. There's a b _ _ _ on the teacher's desk.

4. There's a c _ _ _ _ _ _ _ on the table.

5. There's a w _ _ _ _ _ _ _ _ _ _ next to
   the teacher's desk.

D **JOURNAL**

In my classroom there is _____

_____

_____.

A LISTENING

Listen. Put a check under the correct picture.

1.  ✓ _____   2. _____   _____

3. _____ _____   4. _____   _____

5. _____ _____   6. _____   _____

B MATCHING

1. Open   your name.

2. Write   down.

3. Stand   your book.

4. Sit   the board.

5. Go to   up.

C WHAT'S THE ACTION?

Ask	Erase	Open	Study
Close	Go	Raise	Write

1. <u>Write</u> your name.

2. _ _ _ _ _ your book.

3. _ _ _ _ _ your hand.

4. _ _ to the board.

5. _ _ _ _ _ page nine.

6. _ _ _ _ _ your book.

7. _ _ _ _ _ the board.

8. _ _ _ a question.

A WHAT'S THE ACTION?

Correct	Do	Help	Look	Share	Work

1. <u>Do</u> your homework.

2. _ _ _ _ in the dictionary.

3. _ _ _ _ in a group.

4. _ _ _ _ each other.

5. _ _ _ _ _ with the class.

6. _ _ _ _ _ _ _ your mistakes.

B MATCHING

1. Do   together.

2. Help   the word.

3. Work   each other.

4. Look in   your homework.

5. Pronounce   the dictionary.

A WHAT'S THE ACTION?

Answer	Bubble	Circle	Lower	Match	Take

1. <u>C i r c l e</u> the answer.

2. _ _ _ _ _ notes.

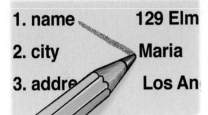

3. _ _ _ _ _ _ the words.

4. _ _ _ _ _ _ the questions.

5. _ _ _ _ _ _ the shades.

6. _ _ _ _ _ _ the answer.

B MATCHING

1. Collect   the word.

2. Underline   the shades.

3. Turn on   the tests.

4. Lower   a piece of paper.

5. Take out   the lights.

A CHOOSE THE CORRECT ANSWER

1.  The clock is (above) below the board.

2.  The globe is to the right / left of the dictionary.

3.  The ruler is between / behind the pen and the pencil.

4.  The mouse is to the left / right of the keyboard.

5.  The teacher is in between / front of the board.

6.  The wastebasket is under / behind the table.

above	in front of	on	under
behind	next to	right	

1. The clock is _____above_____ the board.

2. The computer is _____ the table.

3. The map is _____ the bulletin board.

4. The bookcase is _____ the table.

5. The wastebasket is _____ the table.

6. The bulletin board is _____ the map.

7. The globe is to the _____ of the computer.

A WHERE ARE THEY?

gym	office	cafeteria	nurse's office
coach	teacher	principal	guidance office
nurse	custodian	science lab	guidance counselor

1. The p r i n c i p a l is in the _ _ _ _ _ _.

2. The _ _ _ _ _ is in the _ _ _.

3. The _ _ _ _ _ _ _ _ _ is in the _ _ _ _ _ _ _ _ _.

4. The _ _ _ _ _ is in the _ _ _ _ _ _'_ _ _ _ _ _ _.

5. The _ _ _ _ _ _ _ is in the _ _ _ _ _ _ _ _ _ _.

6. The _ _ _ _ _ _ _ _ _ _ _ _ _ _ _ _ _ is in the _ _ _ _ _ _ _ _ _ _ _ _ _.

18

coach	hallway	classroom	librarian
field	library	custodian	auditorium
office	teacher	secretary	security officer

1. The _t e a c h e r_ is in

   the _ _ _ _ _ _ _ _ _.

2. The _ _ _ _ _ is on the

   _ _ _ _ _.

3. The _ _ _ _ _ _ _ _ _ _

   is in the _ _ _ _ _ _ _.

4. The _ _ _ _ _ _ _ _ _ _

   is in the _ _ _ _ _ _.

5. The _ _ _ _ _ _ _ _ _ is in

   the _ _ _ _ _ _ _ _ _ _ _.

6. The _ _ _ _ _ _ _ _ _

   _ _ _ _ _ _ _ is in the

   _ _ _ _ _ _ _.

Draw a picture of your school. Show the different rooms and label
them.

A MATCHING

1.

2.

3.

4.

5.

6.

eat lunch

brush my teeth

comb my hair

get up

take a shower

go to bed

brush	eat	make	shave	sleep	wash

1. I _____wash_____ my face.

2. I _____ breakfast.

3. I _____.

4. I _____ my hair.

5. I _____ dinner.

6. I _____.

C **LISTENING**

Listen. Write the correct number.

____ take a shower   ____ make dinner

____ brush teeth   ____ shave

_1_ take a bath

A LISTENING

Listen. Put a check under the correct picture.

1. ✔ _____   _____   2. _____   _____

3. _____   _____   4. _____   _____

5. _____   _____   6. _____   _____

B MATCHING

1. feed   home

2. go to   the dishes

3. wash   the cat

4. come   work

clean	drive	iron	study	work

1. I _____ work _____. 2. I _____. 3. I _____.

 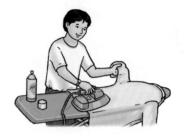

4. I _____. 5. I _____.

D LISTENING: What Are They Doing?

Listen. Write the correct number.

____ feed the baby   ____ wash the dishes

____ clean the house   ____ do the laundry

_1_ drive to work

E JOURNAL

Every day I _____, I _____,

I _____, and I _____.

23

A MATCHING

1.

2.

3.

4.

5.

6.

swimming

reading the newspaper

listening to the radio

exercising

practicing the piano

playing basketball

| listening | planting | playing | reading | watching | writing |

1. I'm ___watching___ TV.

2. I'm _____ the guitar.

3. I'm _____ flowers.

4. I'm _____ a letter.

5. I'm _____ a book.

6. I'm _____ to music.

C **LISTENING: *What Are They Doing?***

Listen. Write the correct number.

____ exercising   _1_ playing the piano

____ swimming   ____ playing basketball

____ using the computer   ____ playing the guitar

25

A WHAT'S THE WORD?

| afternoon | morning | new | night | soon | thanks |

1.
Good <u>m o r n i n g</u>.

2.
Good
_____.

3.
How are you? Fine, _____.

4.
What's _ _ _ _? Not much.

5.
See you _ _ _ _ _.

6.
Good _____.

B MATCHING

1. Good
2. How are
3. Fine,
4. What's
5. See you

new?
later.
you?
afternoon.
thanks.

26

A   WHAT'S THE WORD?

| Hello | Hi | introduce | meet | speak | sorry |

1. H e l l o. My name is Marco.   __ __. I'm Mohamed.

2. May I please _ _ _ _ _ _ to Amber?   I'm _ _ _ _ _ _. She isn't here right now.

3. I'd like to _ _ _ _ _ _ _ _ _ my mother.   Nice to _ _ _ _ you.

B   MATCHING

1. I don't   me.

2. Excuse   repeat that?

3. Thank   understand.

4. Can you please   a question?

5. May I ask   you.

A WHAT'S THE WEATHER?

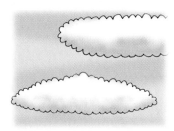

1. s u n n y

2. c _ _ _ _ _ _

3. r _ _ _ _ _ _ _

4. h _ _ _ _ _

5. f _ _ _ _

6. s _ _ _ _ _ _ _

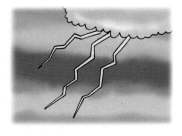

7. w _ _ _ _

8. s _ _ _ _ _ _

9. l _ _ _ _ _ _ _ _

B LISTENING: *What's the Weather Forecast?*

Listen and circle the weather you hear.

1. sunny   (snowing)

2. windy   humid

3. cloudy   clear

4. muggy   foggy

5. drizzling   hazy

6. snowstorm   thunderstorm

cold   cool   freezing   hot   warm

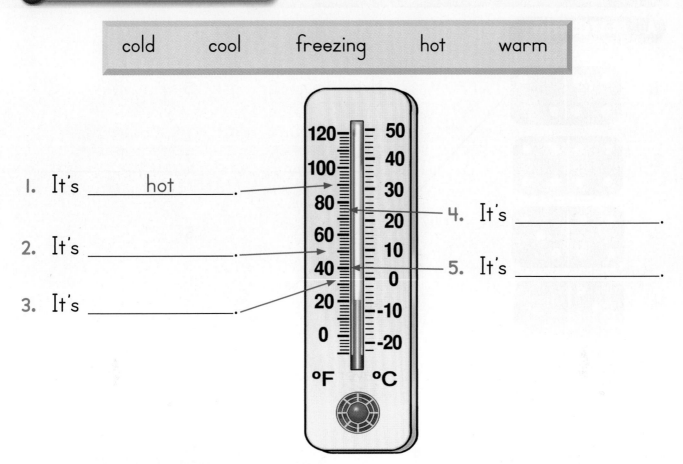

1. It's _____hot_____.

2. It's _____.

3. It's _____.

4. It's _____.

5. It's _____.

D WORDSEARCH

```
B  D  Z  Z  T  Y  S  F  C  L  E  A  R  G
F  O  G  G  Y  L  U  I  L  D  M  U  N  C
I  F  J  R  K  S  N  O  W  I  N  G  X  L
A  R  E  S  G  B  N  T  H  U  V  C  G  O
H  Q  P  B  J  L  Y  Q  U  Q  W  S  O  U
W  Y  H  U  M  I  D  A  L  K  V  O  P  D
A  M  H  P  F  X  E  T  M  W  I  N  D  Y
R  A  I  N  I  N  G  C  R  K  W  E  N  X
M  D  O  X  W  I  A  S  Y  V  C  N  J  Z
```

__ CLEAR   __ HUMID   ✓ SUNNY

__ CLOUDY   __ RAINING   __ WARM

__ FOGGY   ✓ SNOWING   __ WINDY

A MATCHING

1. [domino: 6 | 6]
2. [domino: 3 | 5]
3. [domino: 3 | 4]
4. [domino: 2 | 1]
5. [domino: 2 | 2]

five   5

three   7

six   8

eight   3

seven   6

B WHAT'S THE NUMBER?

1. nine   9

2. four   _____

3. sixteen   _____

4. twelve   _____

5. fifty   _____

C WHAT'S THE WORD?

4   four

6   _____

13   _____

70   _____

100 _____

D LISTENING

Listen and circle the number you hear.

1. (13)   30   3. 17   70   5. 42   24

2. 14   40   4. 16   60   6. 35   53

A MATCHING

1. third	9th
2. ninth	60th
3. first	12th
4. twelfth	3rd
5. sixtieth	1st

6. eleventh	80th
7. eighth	11th
8. fourth	14th
9. eightieth	4th
10. fourteenth	8th

B WHAT'S THE NUMBER?

1. second   __2nd__
2. tenth   _____
3. thirteenth   _____
4. first   _____
5. fiftieth   _____
6. third   _____

C WHAT'S THE WORD?

14th   __fourteenth__

6th   _____

60th   _____

11th   _____

20th   _____

21st   _____

D MATCHING

1. four	fifth
2. five	second
3. two	fourth
4. one	third
5. three	tenth
6. ten	first

E LISTENING

Listen and circle the number you hear.

1. 4th   (14th)   40th
2. 7th   17th   70th
3. 3rd   13th   30th
4. 8th   18th   80th
5. 2nd   22nd   32nd

A WHAT TIME IS IT?

<u>10:00</u>   _____   _____   _____

_____   _____   _____   _____

B CHOOSE THE CORRECT ANSWER

1. (a.) It's a quarter to three.
   b. It's a quarter to four.

2. a. It's seven thirty.
   b. It's six thirty.

3. a. It's five thirty.
   b. It's six twenty-five.

4. a. It's a quarter to eight.
   b. It's a quarter after eight.

C MATCHING

1. a quarter to six   6:30   ten to seven

2. six twenty   6:15   five forty-five

3. half past six   5:45   six thirty

4. a quarter after six   6:50   twenty after six

5. six fifty   6:20   six fifteen

D CHOOSE THE CORRECT TIME

1. (7:00 A.M.)   2. noon   3. noon   4. 10:00 A.M.
   7:00 P.M.   midnight   midnight   10:00 P.M.

E LISTENING

Listen and circle the time you hear.

1. 2:30   (8:30)   4. 5:45   6:45

2. 10:00   2:00   5. 1:30   2:30

3. 3:15   4:15   6. 5:01   1:05

F JOURNAL: *My Daily Schedule*

I get up at _____. I eat breakfast at _____.
I go to school at _____. I have lunch at _____.
I eat dinner at _____. I go to sleep at _____.

A WHAT IS IT?

1.   p e n n y

   1¢ $.01

2.   _ _ _ _

   ___ ___

3.   _ _ _ _ _ _ _

   ___ ___

4.   _ _ _ _ _ _

   ___ ___

5.   _ _ _ _ _ _ _ _

   ___ ___

B WHAT'S THE AMOUNT?

| $.05 | $.12 | $.15 | $.25 | $.26 | $.40 | $.75 | $1.00 |

1. $.05   2. _____   3. _____   4. _____

5. _____   6. _____   7. _____   8. _____

A MATCHING

1.

2.

3.

4.

5.

fifty dollars $1.00

ten dollars $20.00

twenty dollars $5.00

one dollar $50.00

five dollars $10.00

B WHAT'S THE AMOUNT?

1. _____$11.00_____   2. _____

3. _____   4. _____

C LISTENING

Listen and circle the amount you hear.

1. ($35.00) $.35   4. $16.00 $61.00

2. $.05 $5.00   5. $7.10 $71.00

3. $.44 $44.00   6. $14.41 $41.14

A WHAT'S MISSING?

1. Ja_n_uary

2. F_bruary

3. Ma_ch

4. A__il

5. M__

6. J__e

7. J__y

8. A_g__t

9. S__t__ber

10. O__o_er

11. N_____

12. D_____

B WRITE THE MONTH

1. January   __February__   March

2. March April _____

3. June _____ August

4. August _____ October

5. October November _____

C WHAT'S MISSING?

1. S_u_nday

2. Mo_day

3. Tue_d__

4. We_nes___

5. Th___day

6. F_____

7. S_____

D WRITE THE DAY

1. SUN   _____Sunday_____

2. MON   _____

3. TUE   _____

4. WED   _____

5. THU   _____

6. FRI   _____

7. SAT   _____

E MATCHING

1. 6/14/09

2. 4/6/90

3. 1/2/11

4. 2/1/11

5. 3/6/00

March 6, 2000

January 2, 2011

February 1, 2011

June 14, 2009

April 6, 1990

F WRITING

1. What day is it?   It's _____.

2. What year is it?   It's _____.

3. What month is it?   It's _____.

4. What's today's date?   Today is _____.

G LISTENING

Listen and circle the correct answer.

1. (Monday)   Sunday

2. Thursday   Tuesday

3. June   July

4. November   December

5. April 4   April 14

6. May 7   March 7

A WHAT'S THE WORD?

SUN	MON	TUE	WED	THU	FRI	SAT
	1	②2	3	4	5	6
7	8	9	10	11	12	13

SUN	MON	TUE	WED	THU	FRI	SAT
	1	2	3	4	5	6
7	8	9	⑩10	11	12	13

Today	Tomorrow	Yesterday

last	next	this

Today is March 2nd.

1. ___Today___ is Tuesday.

2. _____ was Monday.

3. _____ is Wednesday.

Today is March 10th.

4. March 12th is _____ week.

5. March 1st was _____ week.

6. March 16th is _____ week.

B WRITING

Write these dates in numbers.

1. What's today's date?   _ _ / _ _ / _ _

2. What's tomorrow's date?   _ _ / _ _ / _ _

3. What was yesterday's date? _ _ / _ _ / _ _

C WHAT'S THE SEASON?

_ _ _ _ _ _   _ _ _ _ _ _   _ _ _ _   _ _ _ _ _ _

A CHOOSE THE CORRECT ANSWER

1. a. She lives in a house.
   b. She lives in an apartment.

2. a. He lives in a dormitory.
   b. He lives on a ranch.

3. a. They live on a houseboat.
   b. They live in a mobile home.

4. a. We live on a farm.
   b. We live in the city.

B WHAT TYPE OF HOUSING?

1. h o u s e   2. _ _ _ _ _ _ _ _ _   3. _ _ _ _ _ _ _

4. _ _ _ _ _ _ _ _ _   5. _ _ _ _ _ _ _ _ _

6. _ _ _ _ _ _ _ _

A CIRCLE THE CORRECT WORD

1. mantel
   (bookcase)

2. sofa
   armchair

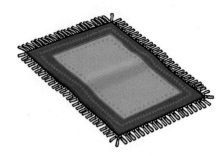

3. rug
   picture

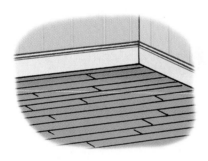

4. floor
   ceiling

5. painting
   window

6. television
   DVD player

B WHERE IS IT?

Look at page 46 of the dictionary. Write the correct word.

1. There's a <u>l a m p</u> on the end table.

2. There's a <u>p</u> _ _ _ _ _ on the sofa.

3. There are <u>d</u> _ _ _ _ _ on the window.

4. There's a <u>p</u> _ _ _ _ behind the sofa.

5. There's a <u>p</u> _ _ _ _ _ _ _ above the fireplace.

40

bookcase	lamp	plant	sofa		window
fireplace	pillow	rug	television		

1. ___rug___

2. _____

3. _____

4. _____

5. _____

6. _____

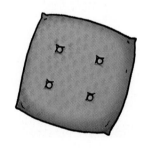

7. _____

8. _____

9. _____

D **JOURNAL**

In my living room there is _____

_____.

A WHAT'S IN THE DINING ROOM?

1. <u>t a b l e</u>

2. <u>c</u> _ _ _ _ _

3. <u>c</u> _ _ _ _ _ _

4. <u>t</u> _ _ _ _ _ _

5. <u>p</u> _ _ _ _ _ _

6. <u>p</u> _ _ _ _

B MATCHING

1. china
2. salt
3. butter
4. salad
5. coffee

bowl
dish
shaker
pot
cabinet

C LISTENING

Listen and circle the words you hear.

1. (butter dish)   salt shaker

2. teapot   pitcher

3. salt shaker   pepper shaker

4. table   tablecloth

5. teapot   coffee pot

6. creamer   sugar bowl

42

D WHAT IS IT?

bowl	fork	glass	mug	spoon	vase

1. _____spoon_____   2. _____   3. _____

4. _____   5. _____   6. _____

E WHERE IS IT?

Look at page 48 of the dictionary. Write the correct word.

1. The platter is on the t a b l e.

2. The fork is on the n _ _ _ _ _.

3. The knife is to the left of the s _ _ _ _.

4. The cup is on the s _ _ _ _ _.

5. The g _ _ _ _ is to the right of the mug.

6. The p _ _ _ _ is between the fork and the knife.

7. The pitcher is on the b _ _ _ _ _.

8. The c _ _ _ _ _ _ _ _ _ _ is above the table.

A WHAT'S THE WORD?

| bed | blanket | blinds | dresser | mirror | pillow |

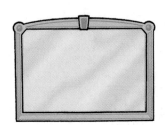

1. _____pillow_____

2. _____

3. _____

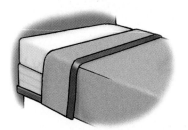

4. _____

5. _____

6. _____

B MATCHING

1. night   radio

2. alarm   spring

3. jewelry   clock

4. bed   table

5. clock   box

6. box   frame

Look at page 50 of the dictionary. Write the correct word.

1. The pillow is on the <u>b e d</u>.

2. The jewelry box is on the _ _ _ _ _ _ _.

3. The box spring is below the _ _ _ _ _ _ _ _.

4. The alarm clock is on the _ _ _ _ _   _ _ _ _ _.

5. The _ _ _ _ _ _ is over the dresser.

6. The _ _ _ _ _ _ _ _ are on the window.

D LISTENING

Listen and circle the words you hear.

1. (blanket)
   blinds

2. mattress
   dresser

3. bedspread
   box spring

4. dresser
   mirror

5. pillow
   blanket

6. alarm clock
   clock radio

E JOURNAL

In my bedroom there is _____

_____

_____.

A WHAT'S IN THE KITCHEN?

blender	dishwasher	oven	sink	toaster
cabinet	microwave	refrigerator	stove	

1. _____oven_____

2. _____

3. _____

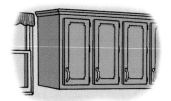

4. _____

5. _____

6. _____

7. _____

8. _____

9. _____

B MATCHING

1. can   rack

2. dish   board

3. garbage   opener

4. cutting   pail

5. tea   compactor

6. spice   kettle

7. toaster   rack

8. trash   oven

46

A WHAT IS IT?

car seat	crib	doll	high chair	stroller	swing

1. _____crib_____   2. _____   3. _____

4. _____   5. _____   6. _____

B MATCHING

Look at page 54 of the dictionary. Complete the sentences.

1. The baby is

2. The baby monitor is

3. The stuffed animal is

4. The stretch suit is

5. The mobile is

over the crib.

on the changing table.

in the playpen.

in the toy chest.

on the chest.

A WHAT'S IN THE BATHROOM?

bath mat	mirror	shower	soap	toothbrush
bathtub	plunger	sink	toilet	

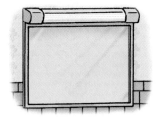

1. _____mirror_____

2. _____

3. _____

4. _____

5. _____

6. _____

7. _____

8. _____

9. _____

B LISTENING

Listen and circle the word you hear.

1. mat   (mirror)   4. toilet   towel

2. sink   scale   5. plunger   sponge

3. shelf   shower   6. cup   tub

A WHAT IS IT?

| chimney | garage | lamppost | lawnmower | mailbox | window |

1. window

2. _____

3. _____

4. _____

5. _____

6. _____

B MATCHING

1.   door knob   garage

2.   letter   lawnmower

3.   television   door

4.   grass   mailbox

5.   car   satellite dish

A CHOOSE THE CORRECT WORD

1. classified ad
   (vacancy sign)

2. lease
   tenant

3. lock
   key

4. fire escape
   balcony

5. whirlpool
   air conditioner

6. trash bin
   moving truck

B MATCHING

1. moving   conditioner

2. parking   pool

3. building   garage

4. swimming   truck

5. air   deposit

6. security   manager

A WHAT IS IT?

1. m a i l b o x

2. _ _ _ _ _ _ _ _ _

3. _ _ _ _ _ _ _ _ _

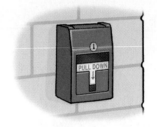

4. _ _ _ _ _ _ _ _ _

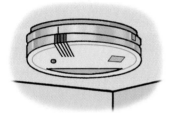

5. _ _ _ _ _

_ _ _ _ _ _ _ _

6. _ _ _ _ _ _ _ _

_ _ _ _

B MATCHING

1. smoke   system

2. fire   detector

3. garbage   exit

4. sprinkler   room

5. laundry   chute

A WHO IS IT?

| exterminator | painter | plumber | repairperson | roofer |

1. _____painter_____   2. _____   3. _____

4. _____   5. _____

B MATCHING: *Household Problems*

1. The bathtub is   broken.

2. The paint is   leaking.

3. The refrigerator is   working.

4. The sink is   peeling.

5. The stove isn't   clogged.

C WHAT ARE THEY?

1. a n t s   2. _ _ _ _   3. _ _ _ _   4. _ _ _ _

A WHO IS IT?

1. <u>l o c k s m i t h</u>　2. _ _ _ _ _ _ _ _ _ _　3. _ _ _ _ _ _ _ _ _ _

4. _ _ _ _ _ _ _ _ _ _ _ _ _　5. _ _ _ _ _ _ _ _ _ _ _ _ _

B MATCHING: *What's the Problem? Who Should You Call?*

1.

2.

3.

4.

5.

The lamppost is broken!

The front steps are broken!

The tiles are loose!

The lock is broken!

The chimney is dirty!

Call a home repairperson.

Call an electrician.

Call a chimneysweep.

Call a carpenter.

Call a locksmith.

A WHAT IS IT?

1. <u>m o p</u>

2. _ _ _ _ _ _ _

3. _ _ _ _ _ _

4. _ _ _ _ _

5. _ _ _ _ _ _

6. _ _ _ _ _ _

7. _ _ _ _ _ _
   _ _ _ _ _

8. _ _ _ _ _ _
   _ _ _ _ _ _

9. _ _ _ _ _ _
   _ _ _ _ _ _ _

B MATCHING: *What Do You Use?*

1. mop the floor   cleanser

2. sweep the floor   ammonia

3. dust   dust cloth

4. wash the windows   trash can

5. clean the bathroom   mop

6. take out the garbage   broom

A WHAT IS IT?

1. p a i n t

2. _ _ _ _ _ _ _

3. _ _ _ _ _ _ _ _ _ _

4. _ _ _ _ _ _

5. _ _ _ _ _ _ _ _ _

6. _ _ _ _ _ _ _ _

7. _ _ _
   _ _ _ _ _

8. _ _ _
   _ _ _ _ _ _

9. _ _ _ _ _ _ _ _
   _ _ _ _ _

B MATCHING

1. electric   spray

2. bug   swatter

3. monkey   roller

4. paint   drill

5. fly   wrench

A WHAT'S THE PLACE?

bank	bakery	bus station
clinic	book store	coffee shop

1. _____bakery_____

2. _____

3. _____

4. _____

5. _____

6. _____

B MATCHING

1. computer   bank

2. money   bakery

3. hair   cleaners

4. cake   barber shop

5. suit   computer store

A WHAT'S THE PLACE?

florist	hair salon	drug store
optician	gas station	grocery store

1. <u>grocery store</u>

2. _____

3. _____

4. _____

5. _____

6. _____

B MATCHING

1. television   flower shop

2. medicine   grocery store

3. bread   service station

4. car   electronics store

5. flowers   drug store

A WHAT'S THE PLACE?

hotel	hospital	health club
library	laundromat	movie theater

1.   laundromat

2. _____

3. _____

4. _____

5. _____

6. _____

B MATCHING

1.   screwdriver   hotel

2.   book   hardware store

3.    clothing   music store

4.   bed   library

5.   CD   laundromat

A WHAT'S THE PLACE?

mall	school	post office
park	restaurant	supermarket

1. ___school___

2. _____

3. _____

4. _____

5. _____

6. _____

B MATCHING

1. eggs   toy store

2. letter   supermarket

3.  teacher   school

4. dinner   post office

5. doll   restaurant

A WHAT'S THE WORD?

taxi	mailbox	taxi driver	fire hydrant
sewer	sidewalk	meter maid	parking meter

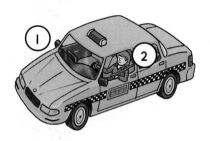

1. _____taxi_____

2. _____

3. _____

4. _____

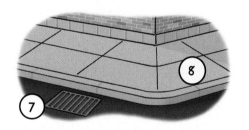

5. _____

6. _____

7. _____

8. _____

B YES OR NO?

Look at page 80 of the dictionary. Answer Yes or No.

__No__ 1. The taxi is on the sidewalk.

_____ 2. The trash container is on the sidewalk.

_____ 3. The police station is next to the courthouse.

_____ 4. The mailbox is next to the fire alarm box.

_____ 5. The garbage truck is under the subway.

A WHAT'S THE WORD?

curb	street sign	pedestrian
crosswalk	traffic light	police officer

1. _____pedestrian_____   4. _____

2. _____   5. _____

3. _____   6. _____

B MATCHING

1. bus — officer

2. public   driver

3. police   window

4. traffic   telephone

5. drive-through   light

C WHICH GROUP?

	People	Places
intersection	pedestrian	_____
pedestrian		
police officer	_____	_____
newsstand		
fire station		
street vendor	_____	_____

61

A WHAT'S THE WORD?

| baby | boy | girl | man | senior citizens | woman |

a. _____boy_____   c. _____   e. _____

b. _____   d. _____   f. _____

B WHAT'S THE WORD?

| middle-aged | old | young |

a. _____young_____

b. _____

c. _____

| average weight | heavy | slim |

d. _____

e. _____

f. _____

A WHAT DO THEY LOOK LIKE?

| black | blond | brown | red |

1. She has long _____blond_____ hair.

2. He has short _____ hair.

3. She has long _____ hair.

4. She has shoulder-length _____ hair.

| bald | beard | curly | mustache | wavy |

5. He has _____ gray hair.

6. She has _____ brown hair.

7. He's _____.

8. He has a _____.

9. He has a _____.

B JOURNAL: *What Do You Look Like?*

I have _____.

A WHAT'S THE WORD?

cold	hot	loose	new	short	tall
high	large	low	old	small	tight

1. _____new_____

3. _____

5. _____

2. _____

4. _____

6. _____

7. _____

9. _____

11. _____

8. _____

10. _____

12. _____

B MATCHING: *Opposites*

1. big — little   messy

2. fast   light

3. heavy   tight

4. neat   little

5. loose   slow

6. wide   light

7. old   narrow

8. good   crooked

9. dark   bad

10. straight   young

cold	curly	heavy	low	messy	narrow	tall	young

1. Is the water hot?

   No. It's c o l d.

2. Is your brother short?

   No. He's _ _ _ _ .

3. Is the street wide?

   No. It's _ _ _ _ _ _ .

4. Is your teacher old?

   No. She's _ _ _ _ _ .

5. Is the box light?

   No. It's _ _ _ _ _ .

6. Is the bridge high?

   No. It's _ _ _ .

7. Is his room neat?

   No. It's _ _ _ _ _ .

8. Is her hair straight?

   No. It's _ _ _ _ _ .

A WHAT'S THE WORD?

clean	difficult	dry	easy	full	sharp
closed	dirty	dull	empty	open	wet

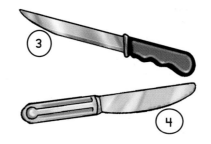

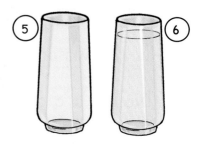

1. _____wet_____

2. _____

3. _____

4. _____

5. _____

6. _____

7. _____

8. _____

9. _____

10. _____

11. _____

12. _____

B MATCHING: *Opposites*

1. difficult   ugly

2. quiet   cheap

3. handsome   easy

4. plain   noisy

5. expensive   fancy

6. hard   married

7. dull   soft

8. rich   poor

9. single   smooth

10. rough   shiny

66

| cheap | dirty | dull | hard | noisy | plain | single | wet |

1. Is the mattress soft?

   No. It's <u>h a r d</u>.

2. Is she married?

   No. She's _ _ _ _ _ _.

3. Is your neighbor quiet?

   No. He's _ _ _ _ _.

4. Is the dress fancy?

   No. It's _ _ _ _ _.

5. Is the restaurant expensive?

   No. It's _ _ _ _ _.

6. Is the knife sharp?

   No. It's _ _ _ _.

7. Is the table clean?

   No. It's _ _ _ _ _.

8. Are the clothes dry?

   No. They're _ _ _.

A LISTENING

Listen. Put a check under the correct picture.

1. _____   ✓

2. _____   _____

3. _____   _____

4. _____   _____

5. _____   _____

6. _____   _____

B WHAT'S THE WORD?

1. <u>s a d</u>

2. _ _ _ _ _

3. _ _ _ _ _ _

4. _ _ _ _

5. _ _ _ _ _

6. _ _ _ _ _ _ _

A CHOOSE THE CORRECT WORD

1. confused
   (proud)

2. angry
   nervous

3. worried
   surprised

4. jealous
   afraid

5. disgusted
   scared

6. mad
   embarrassed

B LISTENING

Listen. Write the number under the correct picture.

_____   _____   _____   ___1___   _____   _____

C JOURNAL

I feel _____ today

because _____

_____ .

A WHAT'S THE WORD?

apple	grapes	lime	peach	plum
banana	lemon	orange	pear	

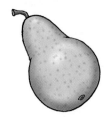

1. _____lemon_____

2. _____

3. _____

4. _____

5. _____

6. _____

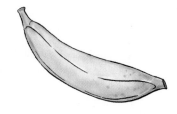

7. _____

8. _____

9. _____

B LISTENING

Listen and circle the fruit you hear.

1. (cherries)   raspberries

2. limes   lemons

3. plums   prunes

4. banana   papaya

5. grapes   dates

6. tangerine   nectarine

A WHAT'S THE WORD?

1. <u>t o m a t o</u>

2. _ _ _ _ _ _

3. _ _ _ _ _ _ _

4. _ _ _ _ _

5. _ _ _ _ _ _ _

6. _ _ _ _ _ _ _

7. _ _ _ _ _ _ _ _

8. _ _ _ _ _ _ _ _ _

9. _ _ _ _ _ _ _ _ _

B MATCHING

1. acorn   potato

2. red   bean

3. sweet   squash

4. lima   sprout

5. brussels   pepper

71

A CHOOSE THE CORRECT WORD

1. steak
   (turkey)

2. ground beef
   salmon

3. lamb chops
   sausages

4. clams
   crabs

5. liver
   roast beef

6. shrimp
   lobster

B WHAT'S THE WORD?

1. s a l m o n

2. c _ _ _ _ _ _ _

3. s _ _ _ _ _

4. h _ _

5. b _ _ _ _

6. l _ _ _ _ _ _

C WHICH GROUP?

| duck | haddock | ribs | sausages | trout | turkey |

Meat	Poultry	Seafood
	duck	

A WHAT'S THE WORD?

1. m i l k

2. _ _ _ _ _ _

3. _ _ _ _

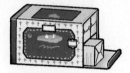

4. _ _ _ _ _ _

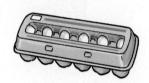

5. _ _ _ _

6. _ _ _ _ _ _

7. _ _ _ _

8. _ _ _ _ _ _

9. _ _ _ _ _ _

10. _ _ _ _ _ _ _ _ _ _

11. _ _ _ _ _ _ _ _ _ _ _ _

B WHICH GROUP?

| apple juice | butter | fruit punch |
| bottled water | diet soda | margarine |

Dairy Products	Juices	Beverages
	apple juice	
_____	_____	_____
_____	_____	_____

73

A WHAT'S THE WORD?

1. s a l a m i

2. _ _ _ _ _ _ _ _

3. _ _ _ _

4. _ _ _ _ _ _ _
   _ _ _ _ _ _ _

5. _ _ _ _ _ _
   _ _ _ _ _

6. _ _ _ _ _ _ _
   _ _ _ _ _

B LISTENING: *Which Food?*

Listen and put a check under the correct picture.

1. ✓ _ _ _

2. _ _ _ _

3. _ _ _ _

4. _ _ _ _

5. _ _ _ _

6. _ _ _ _

C WHICH GROUP?

| corned beef | ice cream | pretzels |
| frozen lemonade | popcorn | salami |

Frozen Foods	Snack Foods	Deli
_____	_____	corned beef
_____	_____	_____

74

A WHAT'S THE WORD?

bread	cookies	jelly	mayonnaise	salsa	soup
cereal	flour	ketchup	rice	salt	spaghetti

1. ___ketchup___

2. _____

3. _____

4. _____

5. _____

6. _____

7. _____

8. _____

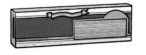

9. _____

10. _____

11. _____

12. _____

B WHICH GROUP?

bread	cereal	mustard	noodles	pickles	rolls

Packaged Goods	Condiments	Baked Goods
		bread
_____	_____	_____
_____	_____	_____

A WHAT'S THE WORD?

1. <u>s o a p</u>

2. _ _ _ _ _ _ _

3. _ _ _ _ _ _ _ _

4. _ _ _ _ _ _ _

5. _ _ _ _ _

6. _ _ _ _ _ _ _

7. _ _ _
   _ _ _ _

8. _ _ _ _ _
   _ _ _ _

9. _ _ _
   _ _ _ _

10. _ _ _ _ _
    _ _ _ _ _ _

11. _ _ _ _ _ _
    _ _ _ _ _

12. _ _ _ _ _ _ _ _ _
    _ _ _ _

B WHICH GROUP?

diapers	napkins	soap
formula	plastic wrap	tissues

Paper Products   Baby Products   Household Items

_____   _____   _____
                        diapers

_____   _____   _____

76

A CHOOSE THE CORRECT WORD

1. customer
   (cashier)

2. aisle
   scale

3. shopper
   packer

4. checkout line
   cash register

5. plastic bag
   paper bag

6. scale
   counter

7. shopping cart
   checkout counter

8. plastic bag
   shopping basket

9. clerk
   scanner

B WHICH GROUP?

bagger	paper bag
cashier	scale
counter	scanner
manager	shopper

People	Things
bagger	_____
_____	_____
_____	_____
_____	_____

A **WHAT'S THE WORD?**

| bag | box | can | dozen | head | loaf | pound |
| bottle | bunch | container | gallon | jar | pint | quart |

 1. a <u>dozen</u> eggs

 2. a _____ of soup

 3. a _____ of flour

 4. a _____ of jam

 5. a _____ of lettuce

 6. a _____ of carrots

 7. a _____ of cookies

 8. a _____ of butter

 9. a _____ of bread

 10. a _____ of yogurt

 11. a _____ of milk

 12. a _____ of ice cream

 13. a _____ of milk

 14. a _____ of ketchup

B MATCHING

1. a jar of   soda

2. a box of   cabbage

3. a bottle of   eggs

4. a bunch of   tuna fish

5. a can of   cereal

6. a dozen   baby food

7. a roll of   paper towels

8. a head of   bananas

C WORDSEARCH

```
L  S  A  P  Q  M  W  R  V  G  Q  N  B  S
S  C  B  E  O  Y  J  L  O  A  F  B  D  D
O  A  R  S  B  Q  J  A  B  L  O  K  O  C
A  N  E  F  P  I  N  T  V  L  D  J  B  B
R  I  H  R  S  Q  D  S  N  O  L  A  D  S
B  R  Q  O  X  Z  N  I  F  N  E  R  V  B
U  B  O  T  T  L  E  B  M  X  P  A  S  T
Q  A  O  L  A  R  J  Z  L  D  O  Z  E  N
A  G  M  P  O  U  N  D  O  N  B  U  E  Y
```

___ BAG   ___ DOZEN   ___ PINT

___ BOTTLE   ___ JAR   ___ POUND

___ CAN   ✓ LOAF   ✓ GALLON

79

A MATCHING

1. Tbsp.	ounce
2. pt.	gallon
3. gal.	tablespoon
4. lb.	fluid ounce
5. oz.	pound
6. tsp.	pint
7. fl. oz.	teaspoon

B WHAT'S THE NUMBER?

1. 1 cup = __8__ fl. ozs.

2. 1 gal. = ___ fl. ozs.

3. 16 fl. ozs. = ___ pt.

4. 1 qt. = ___ fl. ozs.

5. 1 lb. = ___ ozs.

6. 1/2 lb. = ___ ozs.

C LISTENING

Listen and circle the amount you hear.

1. (ounce)	gallon	4. 8 lbs.	8 ozs.
2. Tbsp.	tsp.	5. 1/4 lb.	3/4 lb.
3. lb.	oz.	6. cup	quart

A CHOOSE THE CORRECT WORD

1. stir
   (slice)

2. bake
   boil

3. mix
   grate

4. fry
   steam

5. peel
   pour

6. beat
   cut

B MATCHING

1.

2.

3.

4.

5.

Peel   the turkey.

Stir-fry   the eggs.

Roast   the onions.

Chop   the vegetables.

Boil   the orange.

A WHAT'S THE WORD?

1. <u>t a c o</u>

2. _ _ _ _ _ _

3. _ _ _ _ _ _

4. _ _ _ _

5. _ _ _ _ _ _

6. _ _ _ _ _ _ _ _ _

7. _ _ _ _ _ _ _ _ _

8. _ _ _ _ _ _

9. _ _ _ _ _ _ _ _

B WHICH GROUP?

| burrito | lid | milkshake | napkin | salad | straw | taco | utensil |

Restaurant Supplies | Fast Food

_____ _____ | <u>burrito</u> _____

_____ _____ | _____ _____

C LISTENING

Listen. Write the number under the correct picture.

___ ___ | ___ ___ ___

A WHAT'S THE WORD?

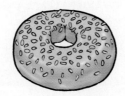

1. <u>d o n u t</u>

2. _ _ _ _ _ _

3. _ _ _ _ _ _ _

4. _ _ _

5. _ _ _ _ _ _ _

6. _ _ _ _ _ _ _ _ _

7. _ _ _ _ _ _ _

8. _ _ _ _ _ _ _ _ _

9. _ _ _ _ _ _

B WHICH GROUP?

biscuit   coffee   donut   lemonade   milk   pastry   sandwich   tea

eat		drink	
<u>biscuit</u>	_____	_____	_____
_____	_____	_____	_____

C LISTENING

Listen. Write the number under the correct picture.

___   ___   1   ___   ___   ___

83

A WHAT'S THE WORD?

booth	chef	menu	table	waitress
busperson	high chair	salad bar	waiter	

1. _____booth_____

2. _____

3. _____

4. _____

5. _____

6. _____

7. _____

8. _____

9. _____

B LISTENING

Listen. Write the number under the correct picture.

____   ____   ____   __1__   ____

A WHAT'S THE WORD?

1. <u>c u p</u>

2. _ _ _ _ _

3. _ _ _ _ _ _ _

4. _ _ _ _ _ _

5. _ _ _ _ _ _

6. _ _ _ _ _ _ _ _ _ _ _

7. _ _ _ _ _

_ _ _ _ _

8. _ _ _ _ _ _

_ _ _ _ _

9. _ _ _ _ _ _

_ _ _ _ _

B MATCHING

1. dessert   glass

2. soup   fork

3. water   bowl

4. dinner   cart

5. butter   knife

85

A CHOOSE THE CORRECT WORD

1. pie
   (cake)

2. nachos
   noodles

3. jello
   ice cream

4. french fries
   potato skins

5. salad
   pudding

6. baked potato
   mashed potatoes

B WHAT'S ON THE MENU?

Fill in these words to complete the menu.

rice	pudding	antipasto	broiled fish	mashed potatoes
jello	meatloaf	spaghetti	baked chicken	spinach salad
nachos	fruit cup	roast beef		

Today's Specials

APPETIZERS:
_____
_____

ENTREES:
_____
_____

SIDE DISHES:
rice
_____
_____

SALADS:
_____
_____

_____
_____

DESSERTS:
_____
_____

A WHAT'S THE COLOR?

1. <u>r e d</u>

2. _ _ _ _

3. _ _ _ _

4. _ _ _ _ _

5. _ _ _ _ _

6. _ _ _ _ _

7. _ _ _ _ _

8. _ _ _ _ _ _

9. _ _ _ _ _ _

B CROSSWORD

ACROSS

2.   4.

DOWN

1.   2.   3.

C JOURNAL

My hair is _____.

My eyes are _____.

My favorite color is _____.

87

A **WHAT'S THE WORD?**

blouse	jacket	shirt	skirt	sweater
dress	pants	shorts	suit	

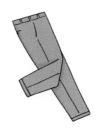

1. _____shirt_____

2. _____

3. _____

4. _____

5. _____

6. _____

7. _____

8. _____

9. _____

B **LISTENING**

Listen and circle the word you hear.

1. dress   (blouse)   4. tie   vest

2. jacket   jumpsuit   5. suit   shorts

3. skirt   shirt   6. skirt   shirt

A WHAT'S THE WORD?

cap	gloves	jacket	poncho	sunglasses
coat	hat	mittens	raincoat	

1. _____cap_____

2. _____

3. _____

4. _____

5. _____

6. _____

7. _____

8. _____

9. _____

B WHICH GROUP?

gloves	overcoat	poncho	raincoat	ski hat	umbrella

It's raining!

It's cold!

_____   _____gloves_____

_____   _____

_____   _____

A WHAT'S THE WORD?

1. <u>s t o c k i n g s</u>

2. _ _ _ _ _ _ _ _

3. _ _ _ _ _ _

4. _ _ _ _ _ _ _ _

5. _ _ _ _ _ _ _ _

6. _ _ _ _ _ _ _ _ _

7. _ _ _ _ _
_ _ _ _ _

8. _ _ _ _ _ _
_ _ _ _ _ _

9. _ _ _ _ _
_ _ _ _ _ _ _ _

B WHICH GROUP?

briefs	nightgown	nightshirt	pajamas	slip	stockings

Sleepwear	Underwear
_____	briefs
_____	_____
_____	_____

90

A **WHAT'S THE WORD?**

| boots | sandals | sneakers | sweatshirt | T-shirt |
| flip-flops | shoes | sweatpants | swimsuit | |

1. ___swimsuit___   2. _____   3. _____

4. _____   5. _____   6. _____

7. _____   8. _____   9. _____

B **WHICH GROUP?**

| boots | leotard | sandals | shoes | swimsuit | T-shirt |

Exercise Clothing   Footwear

_____   ___boots___

_____   _____

_____   _____

A CHOOSE THE CORRECT WORD

1. belt
   (necklace)

2. earrings
   cuff links

3. ring
   key ring

4. wallet
   watch

5. backpack
   makeup bag

6. briefcase
   change purse

B MATCHING

1. wedding   bag

2. change   necklace

3. book   ring

4. cuff   links

5. pearl   purse

A   CHOOSE THE CORRECT WORD

1. (short-sleeved)
   long-sleeved

2. pierced earrings
   clip-on earrings

3. sleeveless shirt
   turtleneck

4. print
   solid

5. striped
   checked

6. plaid
   polka-dotted

B   LISTENING

Listen. Put a check under the correct picture.

1. _____   ✓_____   2. _____   _____

3. _____   _____   4. _____   _____

5. _____   _____   6. _____   _____

A WHAT'S THE WORD?

heavy	large	long	low	short	tight
high	light	loose	narrow	small	wide

1. _____small_____ 3. _____ 5. _____

2. _____ 4. _____ 6. _____

7. _____ 9. _____ 11. _____

8. _____ 10. _____ 12. _____

B MATCHING: *Opposites*

1. long   baggy
2. dark   plain
3. tight   short
4. fancy   narrow
5. wide   light

6. loose   let out
7. small   tight
8. high   low
9. shorten   big
10. take in   lengthen

94

A WHICH DEPARTMENT?

1.  sofa   Men's Clothing

2. ring   Women's Clothing

3.  tie   Housewares

4. stove   Furniture

5.  iron   Electronics

6. dress   Household Appliances

7. TV   Jewelry

B MATCHING

1. snack   counter

2. men's   department

3. water   room

4. men's clothing   bar

5. customer service   fountain

A LABEL INFORMATION

Read the sale sign, label, and price tag. Answer the questions.

1. What's the material? _____ 100% cotton _____

2. What's the size? _____

3. What's the regular price? _____

4. What's the discount? _____

5. What's the sale price? _____

6. What are the care instructions? _____

B MATCHING: *A Store Receipt*

Look at the receipt.
Match the information.

Shopper's Mart

BLOUSE	$30.00
40% OFF	−12.00
PRICE	18.00
TAX	.90
CASH	$18.90

1. sale price $18.90

2. discount $30.00

3. regular price $.90

4. total price $18.00

5. sales tax   40% off

A WHAT'S THE WORD?

a. <u>TV</u>

b. _ _ _ _ _ _ _ _ _

c. _ _ _ _ _

d. _ _ _ _ _ _ _ _ _ _

e. _ _ _ _ _ _ _ _ _ _ _ _

f. _ _ _ _ _ _ _

g. _ _ _ _ _ _ _ _ _

h. _ _ _ _ _ _ _ _ _ _

B MATCHING

1. clock — radio

2. answering — attachment

3. cell — system

4. video game — phone

5. flash — machine

A WHAT'S THE WORD?

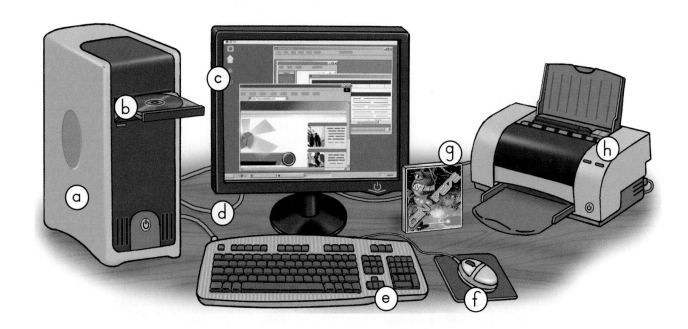

a. <u>c o m p u t e r</u>

b. _ _ - _ _ _

c. _ _ _ _ _ _ _ _

d. _ _ _ _ _

e. _ _ _ _ _ _ _ _

f. _ _ _ _ _

g. _ _ _ _ _ _ _ _ _ _ _ _

h. _ _ _ _ _ _ _

B MATCHING

1. notebook   drive

2. disk   screen

3. surge   computer

4. LCD   program

5. software   protector

A CHOOSE THE CORRECT WORD

1. bankbook
   (check)

2. credit card
   currency

3. ATM card
   deposit slip

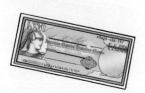

4. traveler's check
   withdrawal slip

5. teller
   account

6. bank officer
   security guard

B AT THE BANK

Your account number is 4159 8673. Make withdrawals and deposits.

WITHDRAWAL APPLICATION

Date _____

_4159 8673_
Account number

CASH WITHDRAWAL	$75.00
CHECK WITHDRAWAL	
TOTAL WITHDRAWAL	$75.00

_____
Signature

1. Withdraw $75.00 (cash).

WITHDRAWAL APPLICATION

Date _____

_____
Account number

CASH WITHDRAWAL	
CHECK WITHDRAWAL	
TOTAL WITHDRAWAL	

_____
Signature

2. Withdraw $200.00 (cash).

DEPOSIT SLIP

Date _____

Account number
_____

Name
_____

Sign here ONLY if cash received from deposit

CURRENCY	
COIN	
CHECKS	
LESS CASH	
TOTAL	

3. Deposit $100.00 (cash).

DEPOSIT SLIP

Date _____

Account number
_____

Name
_____

Sign here ONLY if cash received from deposit

CURRENCY	
COIN	
CHECKS	
LESS CASH	
TOTAL	

4. Deposit $256.00 (a check).

A WHAT'S THE WORD?

1. b i l l

2. _ _ _ _ _ _

3. _ _ _ _ _ _ _ _ _ _

4. _ _ _ _ _

5. _ _ _ _ _ _ _

6. _ _ _ _ _ _ _ _ _ _ _

B USING AN ATM MACHINE

Put the pictures in order. Write the number under each picture.

1. Insert your ATM card.	4. Get cash.
2. Enter your pin number.	5. Remove your card.
3. Select a transaction.	6. Take your receipt.

___   ___   1   ___   ___   ___

C PAY THE BILL

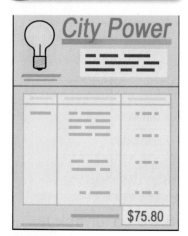

City Power

$75.80

```
                                                          1256

                                        _____ 20 _____

Pay to the
Order of _____  $ [        ]

_____ | Dollars

  N  First National Bank
     1200 West 45th Street
     Chicago, IL 60609

For _____    _____
A012345678A 321 1  123456C 0000
```

A WHAT'S THE WORD?

stamp	mailbox	postcard	air letter	letter
zip code	package	envelope	money order	

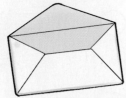  

1. _____envelope_____

2. _____

3. _____

4. _____

5. _____

6. _____

7. _____

8. _____

9. _____

B MATCHING

1. letter   address

2. return   order

3. air   carrier

4. money   post

5. parcel   code

6. zip   letter

A WHAT'S THE WORD?

atlas	magazine	librarian	online catalog
shelves	newspaper	encyclopedia	checkout desk

1. _____librarian_____

3. _____

2. _____

4. _____

5. _____

7. _____

6. _____

8. _____

B WHICH SECTION OF THE LIBRARY?

dictionary	audiotape	DVD
newspaper	encyclopedia	magazine

Reference Section	Periodical Section	Media Section
_____dictionary_____	_____	_____
_____	_____	_____

A **WHAT'S THE WORD?**

ambulance	EMT	firefighter	recycling center
city hall	fire engine	mayor	sanitation worker

1. _____firefighter_____

3. _____

2. _____

4. _____

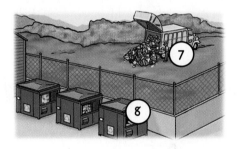

5. _____

7. _____

6. _____

8. _____

B **MATCHING: *Where Do They Work?***

1. police officer   child-care center

2. mayor   dump

3. sanitation worker   senior center

4. child-care worker   police station

5. eldercare worker   city hall

A **WHAT IS IT?**

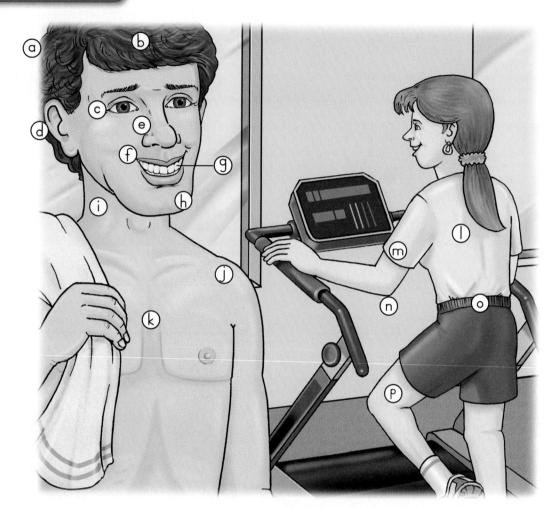

a. <u>h e a d</u>

b. _ _ _ _

c. _ _ _

d. _ _ _

e. _ _ _ _

f. _ _ _ _ _

g. _ _ _ _ _

h. _ _ _ _ _

i. _ _ _ _

j. _ _ _ _ _ _ _ _

k. _ _ _ _ _

l. _ _ _ _

m. _ _ _

n. _ _ _ _ _

o. _ _ _ _ _

p. _ _ _

A   WHAT IS IT?

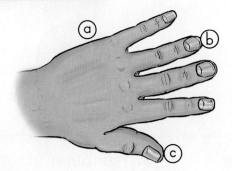

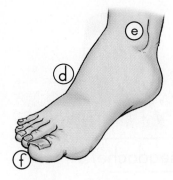

a. <u>h a n d</u>

c. _ _ _ _ _ _

e. _ _ _ _ _ _

b. _ _ _ _ _ _

d. _ _ _ _

f. _ _ _

B   MATCHING: *Where Are They?*

1. throat   foot

2. finger   neck

3. toe   mouth

4. tooth   arm

5. brain   hand

6. elbow   head

C   HOW MANY DO WE HAVE?

1. hands   2

2. fingers   _____

3. stomachs   _____

4. lungs   _____

5. noses   _____

6. toes   _____

7. hearts   _____

8. thumbs   _____

9. livers   _____

10. eyes   _____

A CHOOSE THE CORRECT WORD

1. (headache)
   earache

2. stomachache
   backache

3. sunburn
   fever

4. rash
   insect bite

5. wart
   toothache

6. cough
   cavity

7. cold
   rash

8. sore throat
   stiff neck

9. the chills
   the hiccups

B LISTENING

Listen and circle the word you hear.

1. earache   (headache)   4. runny nose   bloody nose

2. cold   cough   5. fever   cavity

3. stomachache backache   6. chills   hiccups

106

A CHOOSE THE CORRECT WORD

1. congested
   (dizzy)

2. cut
   twist

3. burn
   bruise

4. congested
   exhausted

5. cough
   sprain

6. scratch
   sneeze

B WORDSEARCH

```
V F D T W I Z E C D I F G H
Q H U R T R M D U O R M S F
C Q Z I T W I S T P G N N E
U F Z U V H A D Z Z Y H B V
R A Y R F S N E E Z E Z U E
D I Z Z Y R A I N B E L R W
P N U M E U R S P R A I N Q
Z T N O P W C O U G H X H B
```

__ BURN   __ DIZZY   __ SNEEZE

__ COUGH   __ FAINT   __ SPRAIN

✓ CUT   __ HURT   ✓ TWIST

107

A WHAT'S THE WORD?

1. b a n d a g e

2. _ _ _ _ _ _

3. _ _ _ _ _ _ _ _

4. _ _ _ _ _ _ _

5. _ _ _ _ _ _

6. _ _ _ _ _ _ _ _ _ _

B MATCHING: *First-Aid Supplies*

1. first-aid   ointment

2. adhesive   kit

3. antibiotic   peroxide

4. hydrogen   tape

5. non-aspirin   pain reliever

C MATCHING: *First-Aid Procedures*

1. He isn't breathing.   CPR

2. He's choking.   splint

3. She broke a finger.   Heimlich maneuver

4. He's bleeding.   rescue breathing

5. She doesn't have a pulse.   tourniquet

A CHOOSE THE CORRECT WORD

1. fever
   (heatstroke)

2. the flu
   asthma

3. chicken pox
   measles

4. heart attack
   TB

5. asthma
   mumps

6. depression
   unconscious

7. diabetes
   chicken pox

8. hypertension
   in shock

9. frostbite
   injured

B MATCHING

1. strep   infection

2. high blood   pox

3. heart   throat

4. ear   disease

5. chicken   pressure

109

A WHAT'S THE WORD?

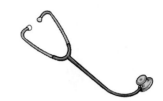

1. s c a l e

2. _ _ _ _ _ _ _ _ _ _

3. _ _ _ _ _ _ _ _ _ _

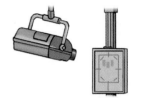

4. _ _ _ _ _ _

5. _ _ _ _ _ _ _ _

6. _ _ _ _ _ _ _ _ _ _

B MATCHING: *In the Doctor's Office*

1. eye chart   blood

2. scale   heart

3. thermometer   weight

4. stethoscope   eyes

5. needle   temperature

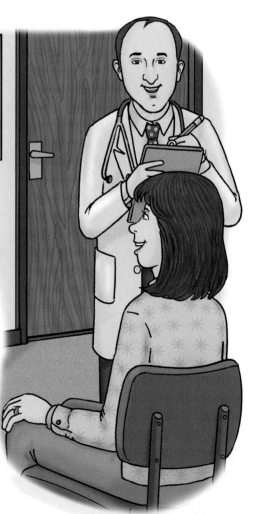

C MATCHING: *What Did the Doctor Do?*

1. She took   my ears.

2. She listened to   some blood.

3. She examined   my temperature.

4. She measured   my heart.

5. She drew   my height.

A CHOOSE THE CORRECT WORD

1. dentist
   (doctor)

2. nurse
   receptionist

3. filling
   stitches

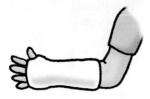

4. cast
   mask

5. drill
   injection

6. brace
   sling

7. crutches
   braces

8. insurance card
   prescription

9. wound
   cavity

B MATCHING

1. medical history   room

2. examination   ball

3. dental   form

4. cotton   pack

5. ice   hygienist

A CHOOSE THE CORRECT WORD

1. (gargle)
   drink fluids

2. rest
   exercise

3. physical therapy
   acupuncture

4. air purifier
   vitamin

5. braces
   tests

6. cane
   walker

7. heating pad
   humidifier

8. acupuncture
   blood work

9. counseling
   physical therapy

B MATCHING

1. drink   bed

2. rest in   vitamins

3. take   a specialist

4. go on   fluids

5. see   a diet

A CHOOSE THE CORRECT WORD

1. (aspirin)
   cough drops

2. nasal spray
   eye drops

3. cough syrup
   vitamins

4. throat lozenges
   antacid tablets

5. ointment
   cold tablets

6. cream
   decongestant

7. tablet
   capsule

8. pill
   caplet

9. teaspoon
   tablespoon

B MATCHING

1. cough   spray

2. throat   drops

3. nasal   lozenges

4. eye   tablets

5. antacid   syrup

A CHOOSE THE CORRECT WORD

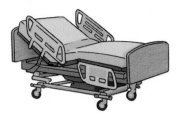

1. bed pan
   (hospital bed)

2. X-ray technician
   lab technician

3. waiting room
   operating room

4. dietitian
   obstetrician

5. medical chart
   monitor

6. I.V.
   EMT

7. surgeon
   radiologist

8. nurse's station
   laboratory

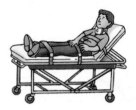

9. orderly
   gurney

B MATCHING

1. medical   pan

2. hospital   monitor

3. bed   gown

4. call   chart

5. vital signs   button

A WHAT IS IT?

1. <u>c o m b</u>

2. _ _ _ _ _

3. _ _ _ _ _ _ _ _ _

4. _ _ _ _ _ _ _

5. _ _ _ _ _ _ _ _

6. _ _ _ _   _ _ _ _ _

B WHICH GROUP?

blush	conditioner	lipstick	shampoo
brush	dental floss	mascara	toothbrush
comb	eyeliner	mouthwash	toothpaste

For teeth   For hair   For the face

_____   _____   ___blush___

_____   _____   _____

_____   _____   _____

_____   _____   _____

C LISTENING

Listen. Write the correct number.

____ comb   ____ scissors   ____ shampoo

____ powder   _1_ hair brush   ____ toothpaste

115

A WHAT IS IT?

1. <u>o i n t m e n t</u>

2. _ _ _

3. _ _ _ _ _ _

4. _ _ _ _ _ _

5. _ _ _ _ _ _ _ _

6. _ _ _ _ _ _ _ _

B MATCHING

1. baby   swabs

2. diaper   powder

3. teething   ring

4. cotton   diapers

5. disposable   pins

C LISTENING

Listen. Write the number under the correct picture.

_ _   _ _   1   _ _   _ _   _ _

A   WHAT'S THE SUBJECT?

1. <u>h e a l t h</u>

2. _ _ _ _

3. _ _ _

4. _ _ _ _ _ _ _ _

5. _ _ _ _ _ _ _ _

6. _ _ _ _ _ _

7. _ _ _ _ _ _ _

8. _ _ _ _ _ _ _ _ _ _

9. _ _ _ _ _ _ _ _ _

B   WHICH GROUP?

biology	chemistry	French	geography	history	Spanish

Social Studies   Languages   Science

_____   _____   ___biology___

_____   _____   _____

A WHAT'S THE ACTIVITY?

1. <u>c h o i r</u>

2. _ _ _ _ _

3. _ _ _ _ _ _ _ _ _

4. _ _ _ _ _

5. _ _ _ _ _ _ _ _ _

6. _ _ _   _ _ _ _ _

7. _ _ _ _ _ _ _
_ _ _ _ _ _ _ _ _

8. _ _ _ _ _ _ _ _ _ _
_ _ _ _ _ _ _

9. _ _ _ _ _ _ _ _
_ _ _ _ _ _ _ _ _

B WHICH GROUP?

band	chess	debate	newspaper	orchestra	yearbook

Music	Clubs	Writing
band		

A MATCHING

1. $3 \times 2 = 6$

2. $9 - 2 = 7$

3. $8 \div 2 = 4$

4. $1 + 4 = 5$

subtraction

addition

multiplication

division

B MATCHING

1. minus $\times$

2. times $+$

3. equals $-$

4. plus $\div$

5. divided by $=$

C LISTENING

Listen and circle the answer.

1. $+$ $-$ $\times$ $\div$

2. $+$ $-$ $\times$ $\div$

3. $+$ $-$ $\times$ $\div$

4. $+$ $-$ $\times$ $\div$

5. $+$ $-$ $\times$ $\div$

D WRITE THE MATH PROBLEMS

1. One plus six equals seven.

$1 + 6 = 7$

2. Eight divided by four is two.

3. Two times five equals ten.

4. Twelve minus seven is five.

(continued)

119

E WHAT'S THE FRACTION?

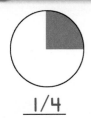    

1/4 ___ ___ ___ ___

F MATCHING

1. one half
2. one quarter
3. two thirds
4. three fourths
5. one third

2/3
3/4
1/2
1/3
1/4

G LISTENING

Listen and circle the answer.

1. (1/3)   1/4
2. 1/4   1/2
3. 1/4   3/4
4. 1/4   3/4
5. 1/2   2/3

H WHAT'S THE PERCENT?

25% ___ ___ ___

I MATCHING

1. fifty percent
2. twenty-five percent
3. one hundred percent
4. thirty percent
5. seventy-five percent

25%
50%
30%
75%
100%

J LISTENING

Listen and write the percent you hear.

1. __50%__   4. _____
2. _____   5. _____
3. _____   6. _____

A **WHAT'S THE WORD?**

line	cube	circle	sphere	pyramid	triangle
cone	angle	square	ellipse	cylinder	rectangle

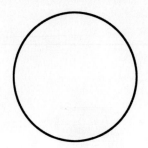
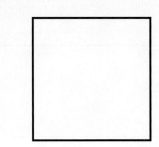
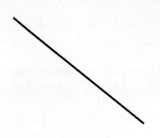

1. ___circle___ 2. _____ 3. _____

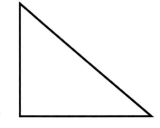
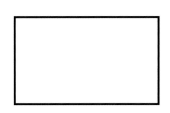
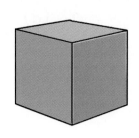

4. _____ 5. _____ 6. _____

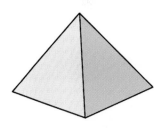

7. _____ 8. _____ 9. _____

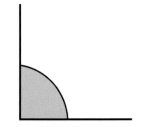
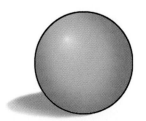
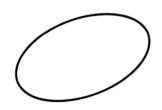

10. _____ 11. _____ 12. _____

(continued)

base	diameter	hypotenuse	length	radius	width

Triangle	Circle	Rectangle
_____base_____	_____	_____
_____	_____	_____

C **WHAT'S THE WORD?**

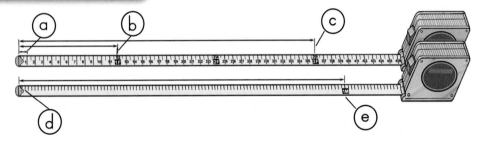

a. <u>i n c h</u>

b. _ _ _ _

c. _ _ _ _

d. _ _ _ _ _ _ _ _ _ _

e. _ _ _ _ _

D **MATCHING:** *Abbreviations*

1. cm   mile

2. m   yard

3. mi.   centimeter

4. km   foot

5. "   meter

6. '   inch

7. yd.   kilometer

E **WHAT'S THE ANSWER?**

1. **2.54 cm =** __1__ **"**

2. **1' =** ___ **"**

3. **0.914 m = 1** ___

4. **1.6 km = 1** ___

5. **1 yd. =** ___ **'**

6. **0.305 m =** ___ **'**

A WHAT'S THE PART OF SPEECH?

> a b c d e f g
>
> They work hard in the new store.

1. adjective   _f_
2. adverb   ____
3. article   ____
4. noun   ____

5. preposition   ____
6. pronoun   ____
7. verb   ____

B MATCHING: *Types of Sentences*

1. Close your books.
2. What's your address?
3. This pie is delicious!
4. I'm studying.

declarative

exclamatory

imperative

interrogative

C MATCHING: *Parts of Speech*

1. eat   article
2. new   noun
3. a   verb
4. car   adjective

5. work   preposition
6. in   verb
7. chair   pronoun
8. you   noun

(continued)

123

1. .	question mark	5. ,	colon
2. ,	quotation marks	6. !	apostrophe
3. ?	period	7. :	semi-colon
4. " "	comma	8. ;	exclamation point

E **FIX THE SENTENCES**

Write the correct punctuation mark.

? ! , . , :

1. My sister's name is Berta.

2. What's your telephone number

3. These cookies are fantastic

4. Please get milk eggs, and bread at the supermarket.

5. My children are in elementary school

6. Our school has three music activities the band, the orchestra, and the choir.

F **THE WRITING PROCESS**

Choose the correct word.

1. Brainstorm (corrections (ideas)).

2. Write a first (draft   declarative).

3. Make (edit   corrections).

4. Get (a title   feedback).

5. Write a (rewrite   final) copy.

A CHOOSE THE CORRECT WORD

1. poetry
   (biography)

2. novel
   editorial

3. invitation
   thank-you note

4. postcard
   poem

5. instant message
   note

6. e-mail
   letter

B MATCHING

1. Thank you for the book.

2. I was a very happy child.

3. It's beautiful here in Orlando!

4. Please come to our party.

5. I M FINE. HOW R U?

6. Crime in our city is a big problem.

invitation

editorial

instant message

postcard

thank-you note

autobiography

C WHICH GROUP?

autobiography	biography	letter	novel	postcard	short story

Fiction	Non-Fiction	Mail
_____	autobiography	_____
_____	_____	_____

A WHAT'S THE WORD?

a. <u>f o r e s t</u>

b. _ _ _ _

c. _ _ _ _

d. _ _ _ _ _ _ _ _ _

e. _ _ _ _ _

f. _ _ _ _ _ _ _ _ _ _

B WHAT IS IT?

| canyon | desert | island | lake | river | peninsula |

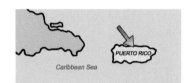

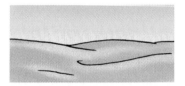

1. _____river_____

2. _____

3. _____

4. _____

5. _____

6. _____

C WHICH GROUP?

| desert | meadow | ocean | pond |
| lake | mountain | plains | river |

Land		Water	
desert	_____	_____	_____
_____	_____	_____	_____

A WHAT'S THE WORD?

1. <u>f l a s k</u>

2. _ _ _ _ _ _

3. _ _ _ _ _ _

4. _ _ _ _ _ _

5. _ _ _ _ _ _ _

6. _ _ _ _ _ _ _ _ _ _ _

7. _ _ _ _ _ _ _ _

8. _ _ _ _ _ _ _

9. _ _ _ _   _ _ _ _

B MATCHING

1. crucible   burner

2. petri   tongs

3. Bunsen   method

4. graduated   cylinder

5. scientific   dish

A WHAT'S THE OCCUPATION?

1. <u>c h e f</u>

2. _ _ _ _ _ _

3. _ _ _ _ _ _ _ _ _ _

4. _ _ _ _ _ _ _

5. _ _ _ _ _ _ _ _ _

6. _ _ _ _ _ _ _ _ _ _

B MATCHING: *Who Uses It?*

1.  saucepan   carpenter

2.  hammer   artist

3. paintbrush   chef

4. cash register   barber

5. scissors   cashier

A WHAT'S THE OCCUPATION?

1. <u>c u s t o d i a n</u> 2. _ _ _ _ _ _ _ 3. _ _ _ _ _ _ _ _ _ _ _ _ _

4. _ _ _ _ _ _ _ _   5. _ _ _ _ _ _ _ _   6. _ _ _ _ - _ _ _ _ _ _ _
   _ _ _ _ _ _   _ _ _ _ _ _   _ _ _ _ _ _

B MATCHING: *Who Uses It?*

1.   broom   hairdresser

2.   computer   custodian

3.   plate   gardener

4.    rake   data entry clerk

5.   brush   food-service worker

A WHAT'S THE OCCUPATION?

1. <u>p i l o t</u>

2. _ _ _ _ _ _

3. _ _ _ _ _ _ _ _ _ _

4. _ _ _ _ _

5. _ _ _ _ _ _ _ _

6. _ _ _ _ _ _ _ _ _

B MATCHING

1. office   housekeeper

2. garage   pharmacist

3. drug store   mechanic

4. hotel   manicurist

5. nail salon   receptionist

A WHAT'S THE OCCUPATION?

1.  t e a c h e r

2. _ _ _ _ _ _ _

3. _ _ _ _ _ _ _ _ _ _ _

4. _ _ _ _ _ _

5. _ _ _ _ _ _ _ _

6. _ _ _ _ _ _ _ _ _ _ _

B CROSSWORD

ACROSS

3.

4.

5.

DOWN

1.

2.

3.

A WHAT DO THEY DO?

1. <u>c o o k</u>

2. _ _ _ _ _

3. _ _ _ _ _ _ _ _

4. _ _ _ _

5. _ _ _ _ _

6. _ _ _ _ _ _ _ _ _

B MATCHING

1. Chefs   mow lawns.

2. Actors   build things.

3. Drivers   cook.

4. Gardeners   fly airplanes.

5. Assemblers   clean.

6. Carpenters   act.

7. Housekeepers   drive.

8. Pilots   assemble components.

A WHAT DO THEY DO?

1. <u>p a i n t</u>

2. _ _ _

3. _ _ _ _ _

4. _ _ _ _

5. _ _ _ _

6. _ _ _ _ _ _

B MATCHING

1. A painter — types.

2. A secretary — paints.

3. A waiter — sells things.

4. A manager — serves food.

5. A salesperson — supervises people.

C JOURNAL: *My Work Skills*

I can _____

_____

_____ .

A CHOOSE THE CORRECT WORD

1. form
   (sign)

2. note
   classified ad

3. job notice
   want ad

4. application
   resume

5. announcement
   interview

6. benefits
   salary

B MATCHING: *Abbreviations*

1. hr.   full-time

2. eves.   experience

3. FT   required

4. PT   hour

5. prev.   Monday through Friday

6. req.   available

7. exper.   evenings

8. avail.   previous

9. M–F   excellent

10. excel.   part-time

A CHOOSE THE CORRECT WORD

1. (time clock)
   work station

2. suggestion box
   dolly

3. line supervisor
   shipping clerk

4. packer
   forklift

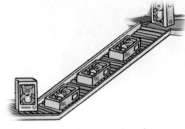

5. conveyor belt
   freight elevator

6. assembly line
   warehouse

7. loading dock
   shipping clerk

8. forklift
   hand truck

9. payroll office
   personnel office

B MATCHING

1. time   line
2. assembly   station
3. work   clock
4. suggestion   belt
5. conveyor   box

A WHAT'S THE WORD?

1. <u>c r a n e</u>

2. _ _ _ _ _ _ _

3. _ _ _ _ _ _ _ _ _ _

4. _ _ _ _ _

5. _ _ _ _ _ _ _ _ _

6. _ _ _ _ _ _ _ _ _ _

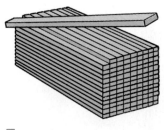

7. _ _ _ _ _

8. _ _ _ _ _ _

9. _ _ _ _ _ _ _ _ _ _ _ _

B WHICH GROUP?

| beam | pipe | bulldozer |
| backhoe | plywood | cement mixer |

Materials   Machines

_____ beam _____   _____

_____   _____

_____   _____

A WHAT'S THE WORD?

1. <u>h e l m e t</u>

2. _ _ _ _ _

3. _ _ _ _ _ _ _ _

4. _ _ _ _ _ _ - _ _ _
_ _ _

5. _ _ _ _
_ _ _ _ _ _ _

6. _ _ _ _ _ _
_ _ _ _ _ _ _

B MATCHING

1. hard hat   eyes

2. goggles   feet

3. mask   hands

4. safety boots   head

5. latex gloves   face

C LISTENING: *Warnings*

Listen and write the number under the correct picture.

___   ___   ___   ___ | ___

A WHAT'S THE WORD?

taxi	ferry	bus stop	bus driver	bus
train	ticket	conductor	bus station	

1. _____bus_____

2. _____

3. _____

4. _____

5. _____

6. _____

7. _____

8. _____

9. _____

B MATCHING

1. ticket   compartment

2. bus   booth

3. fare   stop

4. luggage   counter

5. information   card

A WHAT'S THE WORD?

down	into	off	on	out of	over	under	up

1. _____ off _____

3. _____

2. _____

4. _____

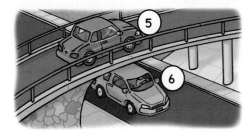

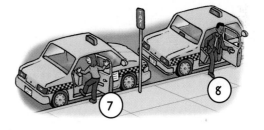

5. _____

7. _____

6. _____

8. _____

B LISTENING: *Following Directions*

Listen and write the number under the correct picture.

___

___

___

___

___

_1_

A MATCHING: *What's the Sign?*

1.   right turn only

2.   no U-turn

3.   no right turn

4.   no left turn

5.   school crossing

6. 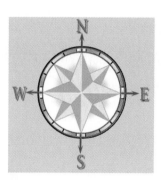   pedestrian crossing

7.   railroad crossing

8.   slippery when wet

B WHAT'S THE COMPASS DIRECTION?

_ _ _ _ _

w e s t

_ _ _ _

_ _ _ _ _

C LISTENING: *Traffic Signs*

Listen and write the number under the correct sign.

___ | ___   ___   ___

140

A CHOOSE THE CORRECT WORD

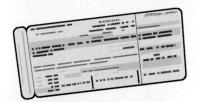

1. gate
   (ticket)

2. suitcase
   garment bag

3. ticket agent
   customs officer

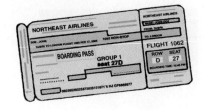

4. passport
   customs

5. visa
   boarding pass

6. security officer
   immigration officer

7. security checkpoint
   arrival and departure monitor

8. boarding area
   baggage claim area

B MATCHING

1. customs   counter

2. security   pass

3. ticket   checkpoint

4. boarding   detector

5. metal   officer

141

A WHAT'S THE WORD?

1. <u>b e a c h</u>

2. _ _ _ _

3. _ _ _ _ _ _ _

4. _ _ _ _ _ _ _

5. _ _ _ _ _ _ _

6. _ _ _ _ _ _ _ _ _

7. _ _ _ _

8. _ _ _ _ _ _ _ _ _

9. _ _ _ _ _ _ _ _ _

B MATCHING

1. yard   market

2. flea   park

3. art   gallery

4. botanical   sale

5. amusement   gardens

A CROSSWORD

ACROSS

5.

6.

DOWN

1.

2.

3.

4.

B MATCHING

1. ping   skating

2. martial   riding

3. horseback   pong

4. inline   tennis

5. table   arts

A WHAT'S THE SPORT?

| baseball | basketball | ice hockey | soccer | football | lacrosse |

1. _____basketball_____   2. _____   3. _____

4. _____   5. _____   6. _____

B WHICH GROUP?

| baseball | basketball | ice hockey | soccer | volleyball |

Field	Rink	Court
baseball		

C JOURNAL

My favorite sport is _____.

My favorite team is _____.

My favorite player is _____.

A CHOOSE THE CORRECT WORD

1. (jazz)
   hip hop

2. classical music
   rock music

3. ballet
   opera

4. cartoon
   drama

5. horror movie
   comedy

6. talk show
   game show

B LISTENING

Listen. Write the number next to the type of music you hear.

___ classical   ___ hip hop   _1_ popular

___ jazz   ___ rock   ___ country

C JOURNAL

My favorite TV show is _____.

My favorite movie is _____.

My favorite movie star is _____.

My favorite type of music is _____.

UPPER CASE LETTERS

TRACE.

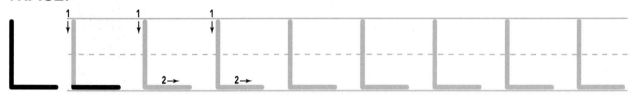

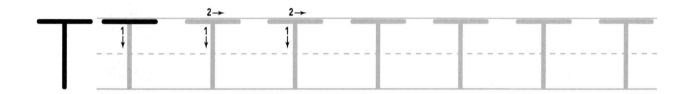

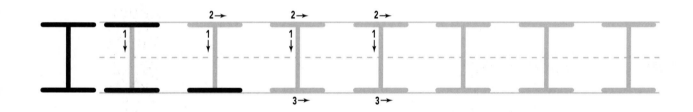

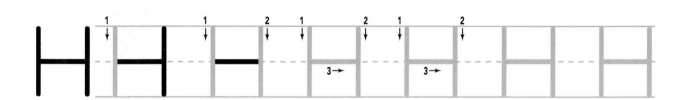

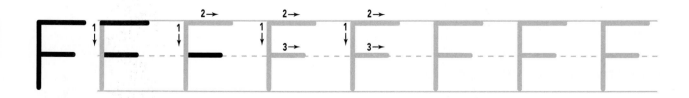

UPPER CASE LETTERS

TRACE.

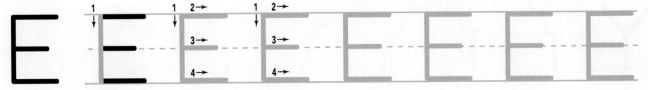

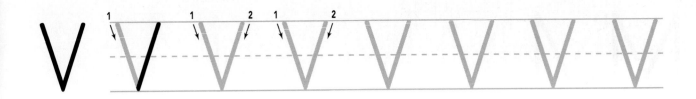

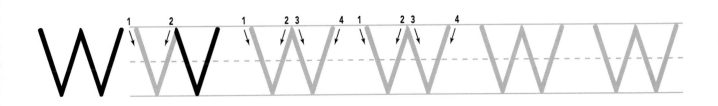

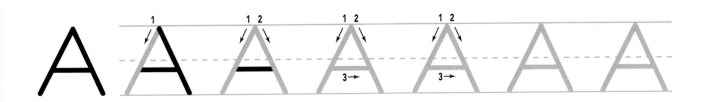

UPPER CASE LETTERS

TRACE.

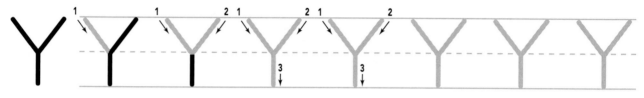

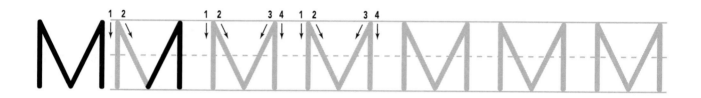

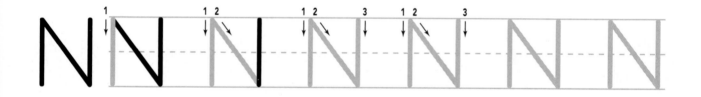

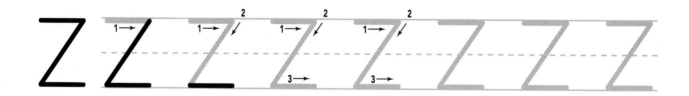

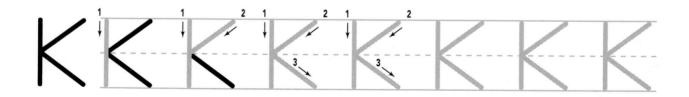

UPPER CASE LETTERS

TRACE.

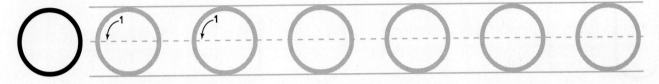

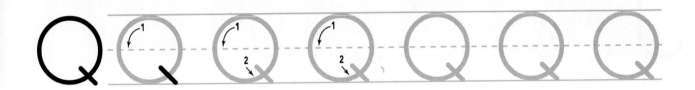

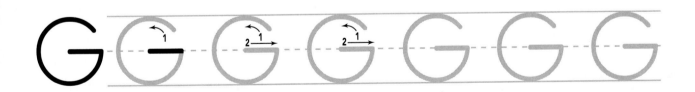

UPPER CASE LETTERS

TRACE.

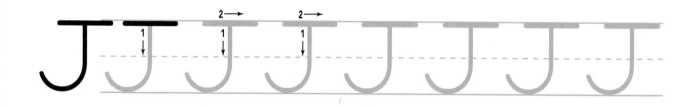

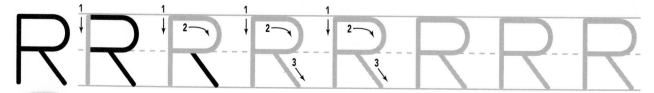

UPPER CASE LETTERS

TRACE AND COPY.

L L
T T
I I
H H
F F
E E
V V
W W
A A
X X
Y Y
M M
N N

Z Z
K K
O O
Q Q
C C
G G
S S
U U
J J
D D
P P
B B
R R

LOWER CASE LETTERS

TRACE.

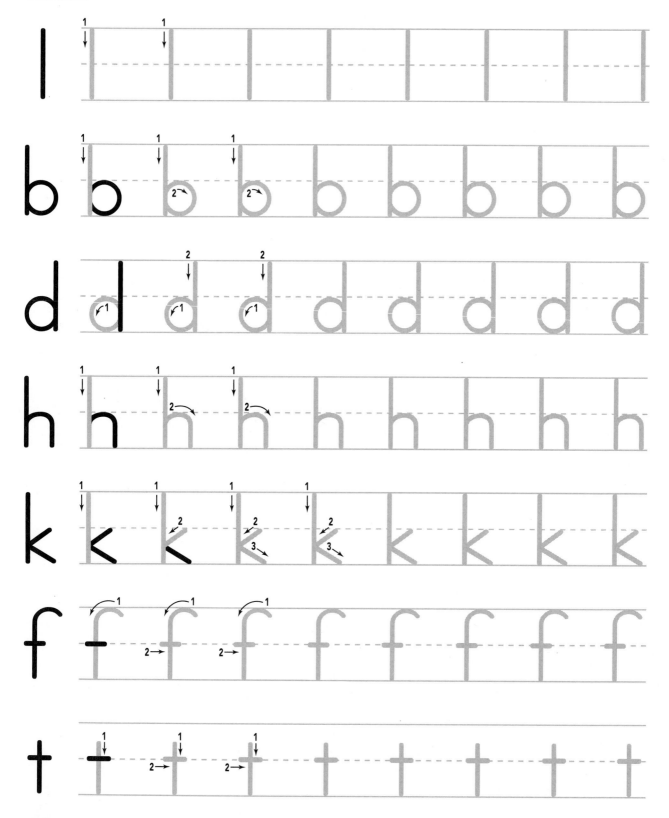

LOWER CASE LETTERS

TRACE.

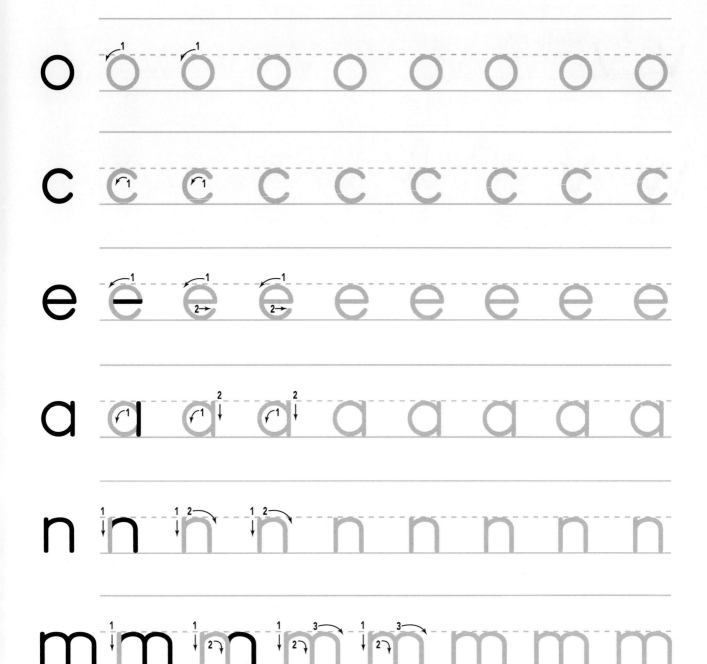

o

c

e

a

n

m

u

LOWER CASE LETTERS

TRACE.

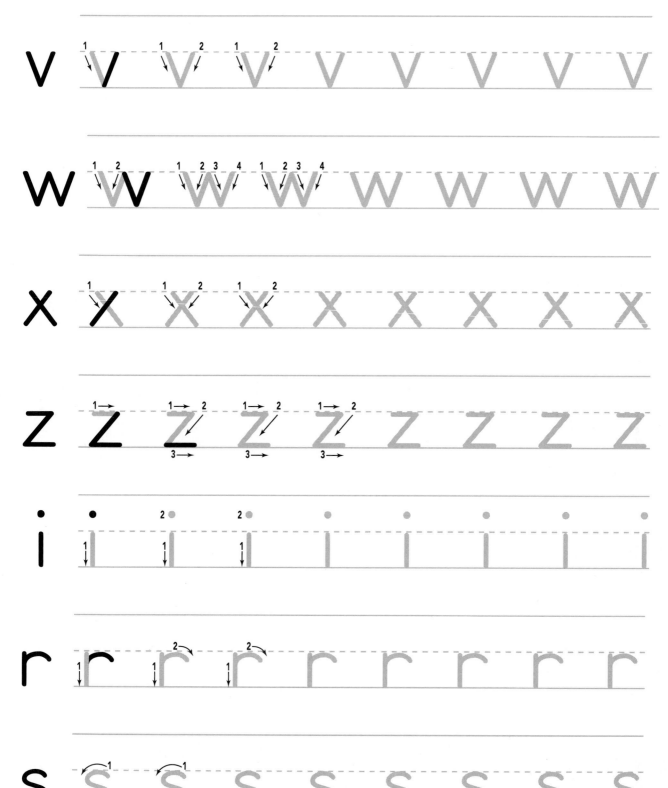

LOWER CASE LETTERS

TRACE.

p p p p p p p p p p

q q q q q q q q q q

g g g g g g g g g g

j j j j j j j j j j

y y y y y y y y y y

LOWER CASE LETTERS

TRACE AND COPY THE ALPHABET.

a a

b b

c c

d d

e e

f f

g g

h h

i i

j j

k k

l l

m m

n n

o o

p p

q q

r r

s s

t t

u u

v v

w w

x x

y y

z z

NUMBERS

TRACE.

1

2

3

4

5

NUMBERS

TRACE.

6 6 6 6 6 6 6 6 6

7 7 7 7 7 7 7 7 7

8 8 8 8 8 8 8 8 8

9 9 9 9 9 9 9 9 9

10 10 10 10 10 10

WORKBOOK PAGES 1–3

A. CIRCLE THE SAME WORD

1. NAME	3. STATE	5. ADDRESS
2. CITY	4. STREET	

B. MATCHING

1. CA
2. 90036
3. GARDEN STREET
4. 323-524-3278
5. GLORIA SANCHEZ
6. 227-93-6185

F. LISTENING

Listen and circle the words you hear.

1. A. What's your name?
   B. My name? John.
2. A. What's your zip code?
   B. My zip code? 22315.
3. A. What's your social security number?
   B. My social security number? 976-24-3069.
4. A. What's your street?
   B. My street? North Tenth Street.
5. A. What's your city?
   B. My city? Sacramento.
6. A. What's your first name?
   B. My first name? Ana.

Answers

1. name	4. street
2. zip code	5. city
3. social security	6. first

WORKBOOK PAGES 4–5

A. WHO ARE THEY?

1. b	3. f	5. c
2. d	4. e	6. a

B. MATCHING

1. father	4. mother
2. sister	5. son
3. brother	6. daughter

C. WHAT'S MISSING?

1. wife sister	4. grandson brother
2. father mother	5. baby daughter
3. husband son	6. grandmother grandfather

D. WHICH GROUP?

Parents	Children
1. father	5. son
2. mother	6. daughter
3. husband	7. brother
4. wife	8. sister

WORKBOOK PAGES 6–7

A. WHO ARE THEY?

1. d	2. a	3. c	4. e	5. b

B. WHAT'S MISSING?

1. aunt uncle	2. nephew niece

3. cousin
   uncle
4. son-in-law
   sister-in-law
5. mother-in-law
   father-in-law
6. sister-in-law
   brother-in-law

C. WHICH GROUP?

nephew	cousin	aunt
uncle		niece

D. WHO ARE THEY?

1. uncle	5. father
2. aunt	6. aunt
3. nephew	7. uncle
4. niece	8. sister

WORKBOOK PAGES 8–9

A. MATCHING

1. pencil	5. pen
2. chalk	6. book
3. eraser	7. calculator
4. ruler	

B. WHAT'S THE WORD?

1. pen	7. marker
2. pencil	8. printer
3. eraser	9. mouse
4. book	10. chalk
5. ruler	11. workbook
6. notebook	12. calculator

WORKBOOK PAGES 10–11

A. WHAT'S THE WORD?

a. map	g. globe
b. teacher	h. board
c. book	i. desk
d. pencil	j. notebook
e. bookcase	k. student
f. clock	l. ruler

B. LISTENING

Listen and circle the word you hear.

1. A. Where's the pencil?
   B. The pencil? It's on the desk.
2. A. Where's the paper?
   B. The paper? It's on the bookshelf.
3. A. Where's the chalk?
   B. The chalk? It's on the teacher's desk.
4. A. Where's the ruler?
   B. The ruler? It's on my desk.
5. A. Where's your notebook?
   B. My notebook? It's on my desk.
6. A. Where's the computer?
   B. The computer? It's on the table.

Answers

1. pencil	4. ruler
2. paper	5. notebook
3. chalk	6. computer

C. WHAT'S IN THE CLASSROOM?

1. globe	4. computer
2. map	5. wastebasket
3. book	

WORKBOOK PAGES 12–13

A. LISTENING

Listen. Put a check under the correct picture.

1. A. Please write your name.
   B. Write my name? Sure.
2. A. Please close your book.
   B. Close my book? Sure.
3. A. Please stand up.
   B. Stand up? Okay.
4. A. Please raise your hand.
   B. Raise my hand? Okay.
5. A. Please put away your book.
   B. Put away my book? Okay.
6. A. Please take a seat.
   B. Take a seat? Okay.

Answers

1. ✓ ___
2. ___ ✓
3. ✓ ___
4. ✓ ___
5. ___ ✓
6. ✓ ___

B. MATCHING

1. your book.	4. down.
2. your name.	5. the board.
3. up.	

C. WHAT'S THE ACTION?

1. Write	5. Study
2. Close	6. Open
3. Raise	7. Erase
4. Go	8. Ask

WORKBOOK PAGE 14

A. WHAT'S THE ACTION?

1. Do	4. Help
2. Look	5. Share
3. Work	6. Correct

B. MATCHING

1. your homework.
2. each other.
3. together.
4. the dictionary.
5. the word.

WORKBOOK PAGE 15

A. WHAT'S THE ACTION?

1. Circle	4. Answer
2. Take	5. Lower
3. Match	6. Bubble

B. MATCHING

1. the tests.	4. the shades.
2. the word.	5. a piece of paper.
3. the lights.	

WORKBOOK PAGES 16–17

A. CHOOSE THE CORRECT ANSWER

1. above	3. between	5. front
2. left	4. right	6. under

B. WHERE ARE THEY?

1. above   5. under
2. on   6. behind
3. in front of   7. right
4. next to

WORKBOOK PAGES 18–19

A. WHERE ARE THEY?

1. principal, office
2. coach, gym
3. custodian, cafeteria
4. nurse, nurse's office
5. teacher, science lab
6. guidance counselor, guidance office

B. WHERE ARE THEY?

1. teacher, classroom
2. coach, field
3. librarian, library
4. secretary, office
5. custodian, auditorium
6. security officer, hallway

WORKBOOK PAGES 20–21

A. MATCHING

1. get up   4. eat lunch
2. take a shower   5. go to bed
3. brush my teeth   6. comb my hair

B. WHAT DO YOU DO EVERY DAY?

1. wash   3. shave   5. eat
2. make   4. brush   6. sleep

C. LISTENING

Listen. Write the correct number.

1. (Sound: bath)
2. (Sound: shower)
3. (Sound: making dinner)
4. (Sound: brushing teeth)
5. (Sound: electric shaver)

Answers

2   3
4   5
1

WORKBOOK PAGES 22–23

A. LISTENING

Listen. Put a check under the correct picture.

1. A. What's your father doing?
   B. He's washing the dishes.
   A. Washing the dishes?
   B. Yes.

2. A. What's your sister doing?
   B. She's studying.
   A. Studying?
   B. Yes.

3. A. What's your cousin doing?
   B. She's working.
   A. Working?
   B. Yes.

4. A. What's your son doing?
   B. He's walking the dog.
   A. Walking the dog?
   B. Yes.

5. A. What's your brother doing?
   B. He's driving to work.
   A. Driving to work?
   B. Yes.

6. A. What's your wife doing?
   B. She's feeding the cat.
   A. Feeding the cat?
   B. Yes.

Answers

1. ✓   ____
2. ____   ✓
3. ✓   ____
4. ____   ✓
5. ____   ✓
6. ✓   ____

B. MATCHING

1. the cat   3. the dishes
2. work   4. home

C. WHAT DO YOU DO EVERY DAY?

1. work   3. clean   5. iron
2. drive   4. study

D. LISTENING: *What Are They Doing?*

Listen. Write the correct number.

1. (Sound: driving to work)
2. (Sound: washing machine)
3. (Sound: washing dishes)
4. (Sound: vacuum)
5. (Sound: feeding baby)

Answers

5   3
4   2
1

WORKBOOK PAGES 24–25

A. MATCHING

1. listening to the radio
2. practicing the piano
3. reading the newspaper
4. playing basketball
5. swimming
6. exercising

B. WHAT ARE YOU DOING?

1. watching   4. writing
2. playing   5. reading
3. planting   6. listening

C. LISTENING: *What Are They Doing?*

Listen. Write the correct number.

1. (Sound: playing the piano)
2. (Sound: playing the guitar)
3. (Sound: swimming)
4. (Sound: exercising)
5. (Sound: playing basketball)
6. (Sound: using the computer)

Answers

4   1
3   5
6   2

WORKBOOK PAGE 26

A. WHAT'S THE WORD?

1. morning   4. new
2. afternoon   5. soon
3. thanks   6. night

B. MATCHING

1. afternoon.   4. new?
2. you?   5. later.
3. thanks.

WORKBOOK PAGE 27

A. WHAT'S THE WORD?

1. Hello, Hi
2. speak, sorry
3. introduce, meet

B. MATCHING

1. understand.   4. repeat that?
2. me.   5. a question?
3. you.

WORKBOOK PAGES 28–29

A. WHAT'S THE WEATHER?

1. sunny   6. snowing
2. cloudy   7. windy
3. raining   8. smoggy
4. humid   9. lightning
5. foggy

B. LISTENING: *What's the Weather Forecast?*

Listen and circle the weather you hear.

1. It's snowing today.
2. It's windy today.
3. It's going to be cloudy tomorrow.
4. It's going to be foggy tomorrow.
5. It's drizzling today.
6. There's going to be a thunderstorm this afternoon.

Answers

1. snowing   4. foggy
2. windy   5. drizzling
3. cloudy   6. thunderstorm

C. HOW'S THE WEATHER?

1. hot   4. warm
2. cool   5. cold
3. freezing

D. WORDSEARCH

```
B D Z Z T Y S F C L E A R G
F O G G Y L U I L D M U N C
I F J R K S N O W I N G X L
A R E S G B N T H U V C G O
H Q P B J L Y Q U Q W S O U
W Y H U M I D A L K V O P D
A M H P F X E T M W I N D Y
R A I N I N G C R K W E N X
M D O X W I A S Y V C N J Z
```

WORKBOOK PAGE 30

A. MATCHING

1. six, 6   4. three, 3
2. eight, 8   5. five, 5
3. seven, 7

B. WHAT'S THE NUMBER?

1. 9   2. 4   3. 16   4. 12   5. 50

C. WHAT'S THE WORD?

four
six
thirteen
seventy
one hundred

D. LISTENING

Listen and circle the number you hear.

1. A. How old is your daughter?
   B. She's thirteen years old.
   A. Thirteen?
   B. Yes.

2. A. How old is your son?
   B. He's forty years old.
   A. Forty?
   B. Yes.

3. A. How old is he?
   B. He's seventy years old.
   A. Seventy?
   B. Yes.

4. A. How old is she?
   B. She's sixteen years old.
   A. Sixteen?
   B. Yes.

5. A. How old are you?
   B. I'm twenty-four years old.
   A. Twenty-four?
   B. Yes.

6. A. How old are you?
   B. I'm thirty-five years old.
   A. Thirty-five?
   B. Yes.

Answers

1. 13	3. 70	5. 24
2. 40	4. 16	6. 35

WORKBOOK PAGE 31

A. MATCHING

1. 3rd	6. 11th
2. 9th	7. 8th
3. 1st	8. 4th
4. 12th	9. 80th
5. 60th	10. 14th

B. WHAT'S THE NUMBER?

1. 2nd	4. 1st
2. 10th	5. 50th
3. 13th	6. 3rd

C. WHAT'S THE WORD?

fourteenth
sixth
sixtieth
eleventh
twentieth
twenty-first

D. MATCHING

1. fourth	4. first
2. fifth	5. third
3. second	6. tenth

E. LISTENING

Listen and circle the number you hear.

1. A. What floor do you live on?
   B. I live on the fourteenth floor.
   A. The fourteenth?
   B. Yes.

2. A. What floor do you live on?
   B. I live on the seventh floor.
   A. The seventh?
   B. Yes.

3. A. What floor do you live on?
   B. I live on the thirtieth floor.
   A. The thirtieth?
   B. Yes.

4. A. What floor do you live on?
   B. The eighteenth floor.
   A. The eighteenth?
   B. Yes.

5. A. What floor do you live on?
   B. The twenty-second floor.
   A. The twenty-second?
   B. Yes.

Answers

1. 14th	4. 18th
2. 7th	5. 22nd
3. 30th	

WORKBOOK PAGES 32–33

A. WHAT TIME IS IT?

10:00	3:30	1:15	6:45
7:20	8:05	12:55	4:40

B. CHOOSE THE CORRECT ANSWER

1. a	3. a
2. b	4. b

C. MATCHING

1. 5:45, five forty-five
2. 6:20, twenty after six
3. 6:30, six thirty
4. 6:15, six fifteen
5. 6:50, ten to seven

D. CHOOSE THE CORRECT TIME

1. 7:00 A.M.	3. noon
2. midnight	4. 10:00 P.M.

E. LISTENING

Listen and circle the time you hear.

1. A. What time does the train leave?
   B. At eight thirty.
   A. Eight thirty? Thanks.

2. A. What time does the train leave?
   B. At ten o'clock.
   A. Ten o'clock? Thanks.

3. A. When does the bus leave?
   B. At three fifteen.
   A. Three fifteen? Thanks.

4. A. When does the bus leave?
   B. At six forty-five.
   A. Six forty-five? Thanks.

5. A. When will we arrive?
   B. At half past one.
   A. Half past one? Thanks.

6. A. When will we arrive?
   B. At one oh five.
   A. One oh five? Thanks.

Answers

1. 8:30	4. 6:45
2. 10:00	5. 1:30
3. 3:15	6. 1:05

WORKBOOK PAGE 34

A. WHAT IS IT?

1. penny, 1¢, $.01
2. dime, 10¢, $.10
3. quarter, 25¢, $.25
4. nickel, 5¢, $.05
5. half dollar, 50¢, $.50

B. WHAT'S THE AMOUNT?

1. $.05	3. $.40
2. $.15	4. $.12

5. $.26	7. $.75
6. $.25	8. $1.00

WORKBOOK PAGE 35

A. MATCHING

1. ten dollars, $10.00
2. one dollar, $1.00
3. fifty dollars, $50.00
4. five dollars, $5.00
5. twenty dollars, $20.00

B. WHAT'S THE AMOUNT?

1. $11.00	3. $30.00
2. $15.00	4. $10.00

C. LISTENING

Listen and circle the amount you hear.

1. A. How much is this?
   B. Thirty-five dollars.
   A. Thirty-five dollars?
   B. Yes.

2. A. How much is this?
   B. Five dollars.
   A. Five dollars?
   B. Yes.

3. A. How much is this?
   B. Forty-four cents.
   A. Forty-four cents?
   B. Yes.

4. A. How much is this?
   B. Sixty-one dollars.
   A. Sixty-one dollars?
   B. Yes.

5. A. How much is this?
   B. Seven dollars and ten cents.
   A. Seven dollars and ten cents?
   B. Yes.

6. A. How much is this?
   B. Forty-one dollars and fourteen
      cents.
   A. Forty-one dollars and fourteen
      cents?
   B. Yes.

Answers

1. $35.00	4. $61.00
2. $5.00	5. $7.10
3. $.44	6. $41.14

WORKBOOK PAGES 36–37

A. WHAT'S MISSING?

1. January	7. July
2. February	8. August
3. March	9. September
4. April	10. October
5. May	11. November
6. June	12. December

B. WRITE THE MONTH

1. February	4. September
2. May	5. December
3. July	

C. WHAT'S MISSING?

1. Sunday	5. Thursday
2. Monday	6. Friday
3. Tuesday	7. Saturday
4. Wednesday	

D. WRITE THE DAY

1. Sunday
2. Monday
3. Tuesday
4. Wednesday
5. Thursday
6. Friday
7. Saturday

E. MATCHING

1. June 14, 2009
2. April 6, 1990
3. January 2, 2011
4. February 1, 2011
5. March 6, 2000

G. LISTENING

Listen and circle the correct answer.

1. A. What day is it?
   B. It's Monday.
   A. Monday? Thanks.
2. A. What day is it?
   B. It's Tuesday.
   A. Tuesday? Thanks.
3. A. What month is it?
   B. June.
   A. June? Thanks.
4. A. What month is it?
   B. It's December.
   A. December? Thanks.
5. A. What's today's date?
   B. Today is April fourth.
   A. April fourth? Thanks.
6. A. When is your birthday?
   B. My birthday is on March seventh.
   A. March seventh?
   B. Yes.

Answers

1. Monday
2. Tuesday
3. June
4. December
5. April 4
6. March 7

WORKBOOK PAGE 38

A. WHAT'S THE WORD?

1. Today
2. Yesterday
3. Tomorrow
4. this
5. last
6. next

C. WHAT'S THE SEASON?

summer   winter   fall   spring

WORKBOOK PAGE 39

A. CHOOSE THE CORRECT ANSWER

1. b   2. a   3. b   4. a

B. WHAT TYPE OF HOUSING?

1. house
2. apartment
3. duplex
4. dormitory
5. townhouse
6. shelter

WORKBOOK PAGES 40–41

A. CIRCLE THE CORRECT WORD

1. bookcase
2. armchair
3. rug
4. floor
5. painting
6. DVD player

B. WHERE IS IT?

1. lamp
2. pillow
3. drapes
4. plant
5. painting

C. WHAT'S THE WORD?

1. rug
2. sofa
3. lamp
4. plant
5. window
6. bookcase
7. pillow
8. fireplace
9. television

WORKBOOK PAGES 42–43

A. WHAT'S IN THE DINING ROOM?

1. table
2. chair
3. candle
4. teapot
5. pitcher
6. plate

B. MATCHING

1. cabinet
2. shaker
3. dish
4. bowl
5. pot

C. LISTENING

Listen and circle the words you hear.

1. A. Please pass the butter dish.
   B. The butter dish? Here you are.
2. A. Please pass the pitcher.
   B. The pitcher? Here you are.
3. A. May I have the salt shaker, please?
   B. The salt shaker? Here you are.
4. A. I really like your tablecloth.
   B. My tablecloth? Thank you very much.
5. A. I really like your teapot.
   B. My teapot? Thank you very much.
6. A. I really like your sugar bowl.
   B. My sugar bowl? Thank you very much.

Answers

1. butter dish
2. pitcher
3. salt shaker
4. tablecloth
5. teapot
6. sugar bowl

D. WHAT IS IT?

1. spoon
2. glass
3. mug
4. fork
5. vase
6. bowl

E. WHERE IS IT?

1. table
2. napkin
3. spoon
4. saucer
5. glass
6. plate
7. buffet
8. chandelier

WORKBOOK PAGES 44–45

A. WHAT'S THE WORD?

1. pillow
2. mirror
3. bed
4. blanket
5. dresser
6. blinds

B. MATCHING

1. table
2. clock
3. box
4. frame
5. radio
6. spring

C. WHERE IS IT?

1. bed
2. dresser
3. mattress
4. night table
5. mirror
6. curtains

D. LISTENING

Listen and circle the words you hear.

1. A. Ooh! There's a big bug on the blanket.
   B. On the blanket? I'll get it.
2. A. Ooh! There's a big bug on the dresser.
   B. On the dresser? I'll get it.
3. A. Excuse me. I'm looking for a bedspread.
   B. We have some very nice bedspreads on sale this week.
4. A. Excuse me. I'm looking for a mirror.
   B. We have some very nice mirrors on sale this week.
5. A. Oh, no! I just lost my contact lens! I think it's on the pillow.
   B. On the pillow? I'll help you look.
6. A. I'm looking for a clock radio.
   B. Clock radios are over there.
   A. Thank you.

Answers

1. blanket
2. dresser
3. bedspread
4. mirror
5. pillow
6. clock radio

WORKBOOK PAGE 46

A. WHAT'S IN THE KITCHEN?

1. oven
2. toaster
3. dishwasher
4. sink
5. cabinet
6. stove
7. microwave
8. blender
9. refrigerator

B. MATCHING

1. opener
2. rack
3. pail
4. board
5. kettle
6. rack
7. oven
8. compactor

WORKBOOK PAGE 47

A. WHAT IS IT?

1. crib
2. stroller
3. doll
4. car seat
5. swing
6. high chair

B. MATCHING

1. in the playpen.
2. on the chest.
3. in the toy chest.
4. on the changing table.
5. over the crib.

WORKBOOK PAGE 48

A. WHAT'S IN THE BATHROOM?

1. mirror
2. toothbrush
3. bathtub
4. sink
5. soap
6. plunger
7. toilet
8. shower
9. bath mat

B. LISTENING

Listen and circle the word you hear.

1. A. Did you clean the mirror?
   B. The mirror? No, not yet.
2. A. Did you clean the sink?
   B. The sink? No, not yet.

3. A. Did you clean the shower?
   B. The shower? No, not yet.
4. A. Did you clean the toilet?
   B. The toilet? No, not yet.
5. A. Did you clean the sponge?
   B. The sponge? No, not yet.
6. A. Did you clean the tub?
   B. The tub? No, not yet.

Answers

1. mirror   4. toilet
2. sink   5. sponge
3. shower   6. tub

WORKBOOK PAGE 49

A. WHAT IS IT?

1. window   4. lawnmower
2. lamppost   5. mailbox
3. garage   6. chimney

B. MATCHING

1. door   4. lawnmower
2. mailbox   5. garage
3. satellite dish

WORKBOOK PAGE 50

A. CHOOSE THE CORRECT WORD

1. vacancy sign   4. fire escape
2. lease   5. air conditioner
3. key   6. trash bin

B. MATCHING

1. truck   4. pool
2. garage   5. conditioner
3. manager   6. deposit

WORKBOOK PAGE 51

A. WHAT IS IT?

1. mailbox   4. fire alarm
2. stairway   5. smoke detector
3. elevator   6. laundry room

B. MATCHING

1. detector   4. system
2. exit   5. room
3. chute

WORKBOOK PAGE 52

A. WHO IS IT?

1. painter   4. repairperson
2. roofer   5. exterminator
3. plumber

B. MATCHING: Household Problems

1. leaking.   4. clogged.
2. peeling.   5. working.
3. broken.

C. WHAT ARE THEY?

1. ants   3. bees
2. mice   4. rats

WORKBOOK PAGE 53

A. WHO IS IT?

1. locksmith   4. chimneysweep
2. carpenter   5. electrician
3. handyman

B. MATCHING: What's the Problem? Who Should You Call?

1. The front steps are broken!, Call a carpenter.
2. The lock is broken!, Call a locksmith.
3. The lamppost is broken!, Call an electrician.
4. The chimney is dirty!, Call a chimneysweep.
5. The tiles are loose!, Call a home repairperson.

WORKBOOK PAGE 54

A. WHAT IS IT?

1. mop   6. vacuum
2. dustpan   7. scrub brush
3. bucket   8. paper towels
4. broom   9. window cleaner
5. sponge

B. MATCHING: What Do You Use?

1. mop   4. ammonia
2. broom   5. cleanser
3. dust cloth 6. trash can

WORKBOOK PAGE 55

A. WHAT IS IT?

1. paint   6. mousetrap
2. plunger   7. bug spray
3. paintbrush 8. fly swatter
4. hammer   9. electric drill
5. batteries

B. MATCHING

1. drill   4. roller
2. spray   5. swatter
3. wrench

WORKBOOK PAGE 56

A. WHAT'S THE PLACE?

1. bakery   4. bus station
2. clinic   5. coffee shop
3. bank   6. book store

B. MATCHING

1. computer store
2. bank
3. barber shop
4. bakery
5. cleaners

WORKBOOK PAGE 57

A. WHAT'S THE PLACE?

1. grocery store   4. gas station
2. hair salon   5. optician
3. drug store   6. florist

B. MATCHING

1. electronics store   4. service station
2. drug store   5. flower shop
3. grocery store

WORKBOOK PAGE 58

A. WHAT'S THE PLACE?

1. laundromat   4. hospital
2. library   5. hotel
3. movie theater   6. health club

B. MATCHING

1. hardware store   4. hotel
2. library   5. music store
3. laundromat

WORKBOOK PAGE 59

A. WHAT'S THE PLACE?

1. school   4. park
2. restaurant 5. supermarket
3. post office 6. mall

B. MATCHING

1. supermarket   4. restaurant
2. post office   5. toy store
3. school

WORKBOOK PAGE 60

A. WHAT'S THE WORD?

1. taxi   5. meter maid
2. taxi driver 6. parking meter
3. mailbox   7. sewer
4. fire hydrant 8. sidewalk

B. YES OR NO?

1. No   3. No   5. No
2. Yes   4. Yes

WORKBOOK PAGE 61

A. WHAT'S THE WORD?

1. pedestrian   4. traffic light
2. crosswalk   5. curb
3. police officer 6. street sign

B. MATCHING

1. driver   4. light
2. telephone   5. window
3. officer

C. WHICH GROUP?

People	Places
pedestrian	intersection
police officer	newsstand
street vendor	fire station

WORKBOOK PAGE 62

A. WHAT'S THE WORD?

a. boy   d. man
b. girl   e. baby
c. woman   f. senior citizens

B. WHAT'S THE WORD?

a. young   d. heavy
b. middle-aged e. average weight
c. old   f. slim

WORKBOOK PAGE 63

A. WHAT DO THEY LOOK LIKE?

1. blond   6. wavy
2. brown   7. bald
3. black   8. mustache
4. red   9. beard
5. curly

WORKBOOK PAGES 64–65

A. WHAT'S THE WORD?

1. new   7. short
2. old   8. tall
3. large   9. high
4. small   10. low
5. hot   11. loose
6. cold   12. tight

B. MATCHING: Opposites

1. little   4. messy
2. slow   5. tight
3. light

6. narrow
7. young
8. bad
9. light
10. crooked

C. WHAT'S THE WORD?

1. cold
2. tall
3. narrow
4. young
5. heavy
6. low
7. messy
8. curly

WORKBOOK PAGES 66–67

A. WHAT'S THE WORD?

1. wet
2. dry
3. sharp
4. dull
5. empty
6. full
7. open
8. closed
9. clean
10. dirty
11. easy
12. difficult

B. MATCHING: *Opposites*

1. easy
2. noisy
3. ugly
4. fancy
5. cheap
6. soft
7. shiny
8. poor
9. married
10. smooth

C. WHAT'S THE WORD?

1. hard
2. single
3. noisy
4. plain
5. cheap
6. dull
7. dirty
8. wet

WORKBOOK PAGE 68

A. LISTENING

Listen. Put a check under the correct picture.

1. A. You look sad.
   B. I am. I'm VERY sad.
2. A. You look cold.
   B. I am. I'm VERY cold.
3. A. You look thirsty.
   B. I am. I'm VERY thirsty.
4. A. You look sick.
   B. I am. I'm VERY sick.
5. A. Are you disappointed?
   B. Yes. I'm VERY disappointed.
6. A. Are you happy?
   B. Yes. I'm VERY happy.

Answers

1. ___ ✓
2. ✓ ___
3. ✓ ___
4. ___ ✓
5. ___ ✓
6. ✓ ___

B. WHAT'S THE WORD?

1. sad
2. cold
3. happy
4. hot
5. sick
6. thirsty

WORKBOOK PAGE 69

A. CHOOSE THE CORRECT WORD

1. proud
2. nervous
3. worried
4. jealous
5. disgusted
6. embarrassed

B. LISTENING

Listen. Write the number under the correct picture.

1. A. You look bored.
   B. I am. I'm VERY bored.
2. A. You look confused.
   B. I am. I'm VERY confused.
3. A. You look surprised.
   B. I am. I'm VERY surprised.
4. A. Are you nervous?
   B. Yes. I'm VERY nervous.
5. A. Are you proud?
   B. Yes. I'm VERY proud.
6. A. Are you angry?
   B. Yes. I'm VERY angry.

Answers

6 3 4 1 5 2

WORKBOOK PAGE 70

A. WHAT'S THE WORD?

1. lemon
2. apple
3. pear
4. plum
5. lime
6. orange
7. banana
8. peach
9. grapes

B. LISTENING

Listen and circle the fruit you hear.

1. A. Do we have any cherries?
   B. Cherries? Yes.
2. A. Do we have any lemons?
   B. Lemons? Yes.
3. A. Do we have any prunes?
   B. Prunes? Yes.
4. A. Do you like the papaya?
   B. Yes. This papaya is delicious.
5. A. Do you like the grapes?
   B. Yes. These grapes are delicious.
6. A. Do you like the tangerine?
   B. Yes. This tangerine is delicious.

Answers

1. cherries
2. lemons
3. prunes
4. papaya
5. grapes
6. tangerine

WORKBOOK PAGE 71

A. WHAT'S THE WORD?

1. tomato
2. onion
3. carrot
4. corn
5. potato
6. radish
7. lettuce
8. mushroom
9. cucumber

B. MATCHING

1. squash
2. pepper
3. potato
4. bean
5. sprout

WORKBOOK PAGE 72

A. CHOOSE THE CORRECT WORD

1. turkey
2. ground beef
3. lamb chops
4. crabs
5. roast beef
6. shrimp

B. WHAT'S THE WORD?

1. salmon
2. chicken
3. steak
4. ham
5. bacon
6. lobster

C. WHICH GROUP?

Meat	Poultry	Seafood
ribs	duck	haddock
sausages	turkey	trout

WORKBOOK PAGE 73

A. WHAT'S THE WORD?

1. milk
2. cheese
3. soda
4. butter
5. eggs
6. coffee
7. tofu
8. yogurt
9. cocoa
10. orange juice
11. cottage cheese

B. WHICH GROUP?

Dairy Products	Juices
butter	apple juice
margarine	fruit punch

Beverages

bottled water
diet soda

WORKBOOK PAGE 74

A. WHAT'S THE WORD?

1. salami
2. popcorn
3. nuts
4. frozen lemonade
5. Swiss cheese
6. potato salad

B. LISTENING: *Which Food?*

Listen and put a check under the correct picture.

1. A. May I help you?
   B. Yes, please. I'd like some salami.
2. A. May I help you?
   B. Yes, please. I'd like some roast beef.
3. A. May I help you?
   B. Yes, please. I'd like some American cheese.
4. A. Let's get some potato salad.
   B. Good idea.
5. A. Should we get some frozen dinners?
   B. Yes. Good idea.
6. A. Excuse me. Where are pretzels?
   B. They're in the Snack Foods section.

Answers

1. ✓ ___
2. ___ ✓
3. ___ ✓
4. ✓ ___
5. ✓ ___
6. ___ ✓

C. WHICH GROUP?

Frozen Foods	Snack Foods
frozen lemonade	popcorn
ice cream	pretzels

Deli

corned beef
salami

WORKBOOK PAGE 75

A. WHAT'S THE WORD?

1. ketchup
2. rice
3. bread
4. jelly
5. mayonnaise
6. salsa

7. cereal
8. cookies
9. spaghetti
10. salt
11. soup
12. flour

B. WHICH GROUP?

Packaged Goods
cereal
noodles

Condiments
mustard
pickles

Baked Goods
bread
rolls

WORKBOOK PAGE 76

A. WHAT'S THE WORD?

1. soap
2. napkins
3. diapers
4. formula
5. wipes
6. tissues
7. cat food
8. baby food
9. dog food
10. paper towels
11. toilet paper
12. sandwich bags

B. WHICH GROUP?

Paper Products
napkins
tissues

Baby Products
diapers
formula

Household Items
plastic wrap
soap

WORKBOOK PAGE 77

A. CHOOSE THE CORRECT WORD

1. cashier
2. aisle
3. packer
4. cash register
5. paper bag
6. scale
7. shopping cart
8. shopping basket
9. clerk

B. WHICH GROUP?

People
bagger
cashier
manager
shopper

Things
counter
paper bag
scale
scanner

WORKBOOK PAGES 78–79

A. WHAT'S THE WORD?

1. dozen
2. can
3. bag
4. jar
5. head
6. bunch
7. box
8. pound
9. loaf
10. container
11. quart
12. pint
13. gallon
14. bottle

B. MATCHING

1. baby food
2. cereal
3. soda
4. bananas
5. tuna fish
6. eggs
7. paper towels
8. cabbage

C. WORDSEARCH

```
L S A P Q M W R V G Q N B S
S C B E O Y J L O A F B D D
O A R S B Q J A B L O K O C
A N E F P I N T V L D J B B
R I H R S Q S N O L A D S B
B R Q O X Z N I F N E R V B
U B O T T L E B M X P A S T
Q A O L A R J Z L D O Z E N
A G M P O U N D O N B U E Y
```

WORKBOOK PAGE 80

A. MATCHING

1. tablespoon
2. pint
3. gallon
4. pound
5. ounce
6. teaspoon
7. fluid ounce

B. WHAT'S THE NUMBER?

1. 8
2. 128
3. 1
4. 32
5. 16
6. 8

C. LISTENING

Listen and circle the amount you hear.

1. A. How much milk should I put in?
   B. The recipe says to add one ounce.
   A. One ounce?
   B. Yes.

2. A. How much water should I put in?
   B. The recipe says to add one
      teaspoon.
   A. One teaspoon?
   B. Yes.

3. A. How much flour should I put in?
   B. The recipe says to add one pound
      of flour.
   A. One pound?
   B. Yes.

4. A. How much roast beef would you
      like?
   B. Eight ounces, please.
   A. Eight ounces?
   B. Yes, please.

5. A. How much cheese would you like?
   B. Three quarters of a pound, please.
   A. Three quarters of a pound?
   B. Yes.

6. A. How much milk should I put in?
   B. A cup.
   A. A cup?
   B. Yes. A cup.

Answers

1. ounce
2. tsp.
3. lb.
4. 8 ozs.
5. 3/4 lb.
6. cup

WORKBOOK PAGE 81

A. CHOOSE THE CORRECT WORD

1. slice
2. bake
3. grate
4. fry
5. pour
6. beat

B. MATCHING

1. Chop the onions.
2. Roast the turkey.
3. Peel the orange.
4. Boil the eggs.
5. Stir-fry the vegetables.

WORKBOOK PAGE 82

A. WHAT'S THE WORD?

1. taco
2. salad
3. pizza
4. soda
5. nachos
6. hamburger
7. milkshake
8. hot dog
9. ice cream

B. WHICH GROUP?

Restaurant Supplies
lid
napkin
straw
utensil

Fast Food
burrito
milkshake
salad
taco

C. LISTENING

*Listen. Write the number under the
correct picture.*

1. A. May I help you?
   B. Yes. I'd like a cheeseburger,
      please.
   A. A cheeseburger?
   B. Yes.

2. A. May I help you?
   B. Yes. I'd like a slice of pizza, please.
   A. A slice of pizza?
   B. Yes.

3. A. May I help you?
   B. Yes. I'd like a hot dog, please.
   A. A hot dog?
   B. Yes.

4. A. May I help you?
   B. Yes. I'd like an order of fried
      chicken, please.
   A. An order of fried chicken?
   B. Yes.

5. A. May I help you?
   B. Yes. I'd like a bowl of chili, please.
   A. A bowl of chili?
   B. Yes.

6. A. May I help you?
   B. Yes. I'd like an order of french
      fries, please.
   A. An order of french fries?
   B. Yes.

Answers

3	5	1	6	4	2

WORKBOOK PAGE 83

A. WHAT'S THE WORD?

1. donut
2. bagel
3. muffin
4. tea
5. coffee
6. pancakes
7. waffles
8. lemonade
9. toast

B. WHICH GROUP?

eat
biscuit
donut
pastry
sandwich

drink
coffee
lemonade
milk
tea

C. LISTENING

*Listen. Write the number under the
correct picture.*

1. A. May I help you?
   B. Yes. I'd like a muffin, please.
   A. A muffin?
   B. Yes.

2. A. May I help you?
   B. Yes. I'd like a tuna fish sandwich,
      please.
   A. A tuna fish sandwich?
   B. Yes.

3. A. I'd like an order of pancakes, please.
   B. An order of pancakes?
   A. Yes.
4. A. I'll have a medium-size iced tea, please.
   B. A medium-size iced tea?
   A. Yes.
5. A. I'd like a bagel, please.
   B. A bagel?
   A. Yes.
6. A. Anything to drink?
   B. Yes. I'll have a small lemonade.
   A. A small lemonade?
   B. Yes.

Answers

2   4   1   6   3   5

WORKBOOK PAGE 84

A. WHAT'S THE WORD?

1. booth
2. waitress
3. menu
4. chef
5. waiter
6. salad bar
7. high chair
8. table
9. busperson

B. LISTENING

Listen. Write the number under the correct picture.

1. A. Do you have any job openings?
   B. Yes. We're looking for a busperson.
   A. A busperson?
   B. Yes.
2. A. Do you have any job openings?
   B. Yes. We're looking for a waitress.
   A. A waitress?
   B. Yes.
3. A. Do you have any job openings?
   B. Yes. We're looking for a host or hostess.
   A. A host or hostess?
   B. Yes.
4. A. Do you have any job openings?
   B. Yes. We're looking for a chef.
   A. A chef?
   B. Yes.
5. A. Do you have any job openings?
   B. Yes. We're looking for a waiter.
   A. A waiter?
   B. Yes.

Answers

4   2   5   1   3

WORKBOOK PAGE 85

A. WHAT'S THE WORD?

1. cup
2. tray
3. napkin
4. knife
5. check
6. dishwasher
7. soup spoon
8. water glass
9. dinner plate

B. MATCHING

1. cart
2. bowl
3. glass
4. fork
5. knife

WORKBOOK PAGE 86

A. CHOOSE THE CORRECT WORD

1. cake
2. nachos
3. jello
4. potato skins
5. salad
6. baked potato

B. WHAT'S ON THE MENU?

Appetizer
nachos
fruit cup
Salads
antipasto
spinach salad

Entrees
meatloaf
spaghetti
roast beef
broiled fish
baked chicken

Side Dishes
rice
mashed potatoes

Desserts
jello
pudding

WORKBOOK PAGE 87

A. WHAT'S THE COLOR?

1. red
2. blue
3. pink
4. brown
5. green
6. white
7. black
8. yellow
9. orange

B. CROSSWORD

(See page 172.)

WORKBOOK PAGE 88

A. WHAT'S THE WORD?

1. shirt
2. pants
3. blouse
4. jacket
5. skirt
6. suit
7. dress
8. shorts
9. sweater

B. LISTENING

Listen and circle the word you hear.

1. A. Do you like my new blouse?
   B. Yes. It's a very nice blouse.
2. A. Do you like my new jacket?
   B. Yes. It's a very nice jacket.
3. A. Do you like my new shirt?
   B. Yes. It's a very nice shirt.
4. A. Do you like my new tie?
   B. Yes. It's a very nice tie.
5. A. Do you like my new suit?
   B. Yes. It's a very nice suit.
6. A. Do you like my new skirt?
   B. Yes. It's a very nice skirt.

Answers

1. blouse
2. jacket
3. shirt
4. tie
5. suit
6. skirt

WORKBOOK PAGE 89

A. WHAT'S THE WORD?

1. cap
2. jacket
3. hat
4. poncho
5. raincoat
6. gloves
7. coat
8. mittens
9. sunglasses

B. WHICH GROUP?

It's raining!
poncho
raincoat
umbrella

It's cold!
gloves
overcoat
ski hat

WORKBOOK PAGE 90

A. WHAT'S THE WORD?

1. stockings
2. pajamas
3. socks
4. slippers
5. bathrobe
6. nightgown
7. knee socks
8. boxer shorts
9. long underwear

B. WHICH GROUP?

Sleepwear
nightgown
nightshirt
pajamas

Underwear
briefs
slip
stockings

WORKBOOK PAGE 91

A. WHAT'S THE WORD?

1. swimsuit
2. sneakers
3. boots
4. sweatshirt
5. T-shirt
6. shoes
7. sandals
8. sweatpants
9. flip-flops

B. WHICH GROUP?

Exercise Clothing
leotard
swimsuit
T-shirt

Footwear
boots
sandals
shoes

WORKBOOK PAGE 92

A. CHOOSE THE CORRECT WORD

1. necklace
2. earrings
3. ring
4. watch
5. backpack
6. change purse

B. MATCHING

1. ring
2. purse
3. bag
4. links
5. necklace

WORKBOOK PAGE 93

A. CHOOSE THE CORRECT WORD

1. short-sleeved
2. clip-on earrings
3. turtleneck
4. print
5. striped
6. polka-dotted

B. LISTENING

Listen. Put a check under the correct picture.

1. A. May I help you?
   B. Yes, please. I'm looking for pierced earrings.
   A. Pierced earrings?
   B. Yes.
2. A. What kind of shirt are you looking for?
   B. I'm looking for a plaid shirt.
   A. A plaid shirt?
   B. Yes.
3. A. May I help you?
   B. Yes. I'm looking for a turtleneck shirt.

(continued)

A. A turtleneck shirt?
B. Yes.
4. A. How do you like this short-sleeved shirt?
   B. It's very nice.
5. A. How do you like this blue and white striped shirt?
   B. It's very nice.
6. A. May I help you?
   B. Yes, please. I'm looking for a polka-dotted blouse.

Answers
1. ___ ✓
2. ___ ✓
3. ✓ ___
4. ___ ✓
5. ✓ ___
6. ___ ✓

WORKBOOK PAGE 94

A. WHAT'S THE WORD?
1. small
2. large
3. tight
4. loose
5. light
6. heavy
7. short
8. long
9. wide
10. narrow
11. low
12. high

B. MATCHING: Opposites
1. short
2. light
3. baggy
4. plain
5. narrow
6. tight
7. big
8. low
9. lengthen
10. let out

WORKBOOK PAGE 95

A. WHICH DEPARTMENT?
1. Furniture
2. Jewelry
3. Men's Clothing
4. Household Appliances
5. Housewares
6. Women's Clothing
7. Electronics

B. MATCHING
1. bar
2. room
3. fountain
4. department
5. counter

WORKBOOK PAGE 96

A. LABEL INFORMATION
1. 100% cotton
2. Small
3. $40.00
4. 30% off
5. $28.00
6. Wash in Cold Water

B. MATCHING: A Store Receipt
1. $18.00
2. 40% off
3. $30.00
4. $18.90
5. $.90

WORKBOOK PAGE 97

A. WHAT'S THE WORD?
a. TV
b. camcorder
c. radio
d. headphones
e. stereo system
f. speaker
g. DVD player
h. clock radio

B. MATCHING
1. radio
2. machine
3. phone
4. system
5. attachment

WORKBOOK PAGE 98

A. WHAT'S THE WORD?
a. computer
b. CD-ROM
c. monitor
d. cable
e. keyboard
f. mouse
g. computer game
h. printer

B. MATCHING
1. computer
2. drive
3. protector
4. screen
5. program

WORKBOOK PAGE 99

A. CHOOSE THE CORRECT WORD
1. check
2. credit card
3. deposit slip
4. traveler's check
5. teller
6. security guard

B. AT THE BANK

(See page 172.)

WORKBOOK PAGE 100

A. WHAT'S THE WORD?
1. bill
2. check
3. checkbook
4. cash
5. ATM card
6. money order

B. USING AN ATM MACHINE
2 5 1 4 6 3

C. PAY THE BILL

(See page 172.)

WORKBOOK PAGE 101

A. WHAT'S THE WORD?
1. envelope
2. postcard
3. stamp
4. letter
5. package
6. mailbox
7. air letter
8. zip code
9. money order

B. MATCHING
1. carrier
2. address
3. letter
4. order
5. post
6. code

WORKBOOK PAGE 102

A. WHAT'S THE WORD?
1. librarian
2. checkout desk
3. atlas
4. encyclopedia
5. shelves
6. online catalog
7. newspaper
8. magazine

B. WHICH SECTION OF THE LIBRARY?

Reference Section
dictionary
encyclopedia

Periodical Section
newspaper
magazine

Media Section
audiotape
DVD

WORKBOOK PAGE 103

A. WHAT'S THE WORD?
1. firefighter
2. fire engine
3. EMT
4. ambulance
5. mayor
6. city hall
7. sanitation worker
8. recycling center

B. MATCHING: Where Do They Work?
1. police station
2. city hall
3. dump
4. child-care center
5. senior center

WORKBOOK PAGE 104

A. WHAT IS IT?
a. head
b. hair
c. eye
d. ear
e. nose
f. mouth
g. teeth
h. chin
i. neck
j. shoulder
k. chest
l. back
m. arm
n. elbow
o. waist
p. leg

WORKBOOK PAGE 105

A. WHAT IS IT?
a. hand
b. finger
c. thumb
d. foot
e. ankle
f. toe

B. MATCHING: Where Are They?
1. neck
2. hand
3. foot
4. mouth
5. head
6. arm

C. HOW MANY DO WE HAVE?
1. 2   3. 1   5. 1   7. 1   9. 1
2. 10 4. 2   6. 10 8. 2   10. 2

WORKBOOK PAGE 106

A. CHOOSE THE CORRECT WORD
1. headache
2. stomachache
3. fever
4. insect bite
5. toothache
6. cough
7. cold
8. stiff neck
9. the chills

B. LISTENING

Listen and circle the word you hear.

1. A. What's the matter?
   B. I have a headache.
   A. A headache? I'm sorry to hear that.
2. A. What's the matter?
   B. I have a cold.
   A. A cold? I'm sorry to hear that.
3. A. What's the matter?
   B. I have a stomachache.
   A. A stomachache? I'm sorry to hear that.
4. A. What's the matter?
   B. I have a bloody nose.
   A. A bloody nose? I'm sorry to hear that.
5. A. What's the matter?
   B. I have a fever.
   A. A fever? I'm sorry to hear that.
6. A. What's the matter?
   B. I have the hiccups.
   A. The hiccups? I'm sorry to hear that.

1. headache
2. cold
3. stomachache
4. bloody nose
5. fever
6. hiccups

WORKBOOK PAGE 107

A. CHOOSE THE CORRECT WORD

1. dizzy
2. cut
3. burn
4. exhausted
5. cough
6. sneeze

B. WORDSEARCH

```
V F D T W I Z E C D I F G H
Q H U R T R M D U O R M S F
C Q Z I T W I S T P G N N E
U F Z U V H A D Z Z Y H B V
R A Y R F S N E E Z E Z U E
D I Z Z Y R A I N B E L R W
P N U M E U R S P R A I N Q
Z T N O P W C O U G H X H B
```

WORKBOOK PAGE 108

A. WHAT'S THE WORD?

1. bandage
2. gauze
3. tweezers
4. aspirin
5. splint
6. sterile pad

B. MATCHING: First-Aid Supplies

1. kit
2. tape
3. ointment
4. peroxide
5. pain reliever

C. MATCHING: First-Aid Procedures

1. rescue breathing
2. Heimlich maneuver
3. splint
4. tourniquet
5. CPR

WORKBOOK PAGE 109

A. CHOOSE THE CORRECT WORD

1. heatstroke
2. the flu
3. measles
4. heart attack
5. asthma
6. unconscious
7. chicken pox
8. in shock
9. frostbite

B. MATCHING

1. throat
2. pressure
3. disease
4. infection
5. pox

WORKBOOK PAGE 110

A. WHAT'S THE WORD?

1. scale
2. thermometer
3. stethoscope
4. needle
5. eye chart
6. X-ray machine

B. MATCHING: In the Doctor's Office

1. eyes
2. weight
3. temperature
4. heart
5. blood

C. MATCHING: What Did the Doctor Do?

1. my temperature.
2. my heart.
3. my ears.
4. my height.
5. some blood.

WORKBOOK PAGE 111

A. CHOOSE THE CORRECT WORD

1. doctor
2. nurse
3. stitches
4. cast
5. injection
6. sling
7. crutches
8. prescription
9. wound

B. MATCHING

1. form
2. room
3. hygienist
4. ball
5. pack

WORKBOOK PAGE 112

A. CHOOSE THE CORRECT WORD

1. gargle
2. exercise
3. acupuncture
4. air purifier
5. braces
6. walker
7. heating pad
8. blood work
9. counseling

B. MATCHING

1. fluids
2. bed
3. vitamins
4. a diet
5. a specialist

WORKBOOK PAGE 113

A. CHOOSE THE CORRECT WORD

1. aspirin
2. eye drops
3. vitamins
4. antacid tablets
5. cold tablets
6. cream
7. capsule
8. pill
9. tablespoon

B. MATCHING

1. syrup
2. lozenges
3. spray
4. drops
5. tablets

WORKBOOK PAGE 114

A. CHOOSE THE CORRECT WORD

1. hospital bed
2. X-ray technician
3. operating room
4. obstetrician
5. medical chart
6. I.V.
7. surgeon
8. laboratory
9. gurney

B. MATCHING

1. chart
2. gown
3. pan
4. button
5. monitor

WORKBOOK PAGE 115

A. WHAT IS IT?

1. comb
2. razor
3. toothbrush
4. shampoo
5. scissors
6. hair brush

B. WHICH GROUP?

For teeth	For hair	For the face
dental floss	brush	blush
mouthwash	comb	eyeliner
toothbrush	conditioner	lipstick
toothpaste	shampoo	mascara

C. LISTENING

Listen. Write the correct number.

1. A. Excuse me. I'm looking for a hair brush.
   B. Hair brushes are in the next aisle.
   A. Thank you.

2. A. Excuse me. Where can I find shampoo?
   B. It's in the next aisle.
   A. Thank you.

3. A. Excuse me. I'm looking for a comb.
   B. Combs are in the next aisle.
   A. Thanks.

4. A. Where can I find powder?
   B. Powder is in aisle three.
   A. Thank you.

5. A. May I help you?
   B. Yes. I'm looking for toothpaste.
   A. Toothpaste is in aisle two.
   B. Thanks.

6. A. Excuse me. Where can I find scissors?
   B. Scissors? They're in the next aisle.
   A. Thank you.

Answers

3 6 2
4 1 5

WORKBOOK PAGE 116

A. WHAT IS IT?

1. ointment
2. bib
3. bottle
4. nipple
5. pacifier
6. baby food

B. MATCHING

1. powder
2. pins
3. ring
4. swabs
5. diapers

C. LISTENING

Listen. Write the number under the correct picture.

1. A. Where's the ointment?
   B. The ointment? It's on the changing table.

2. A. Where are the baby wipes?
   B. The baby wipes? They're on the changing table.

3. A. Where are the diaper pins?
   B. The diaper pins? They're on the changing table.

4. A. Where's the pacifier?
   B. The pacifier? It's in the crib.

5. A. Where's the bib?
   B. The bib? It's in the kitchen.

6. A. Where's the baby shampoo?
   B. The baby shampoo? It's on the changing table.

Answers

2 6 1 4 3 5

WORKBOOK PAGE 117

A. WHAT'S THE SUBJECT?

1. health
2. math
3. art
4. history
5. science
6. music
7. French
8. chemistry
9. geography

B. WHICH GROUP?

Social Studies	Languages
geography	French
history	Spanish

Science
biology
chemistry

WORKBOOK PAGE 118

A. WHAT'S THE ACTIVITY?

1. choir
2. band
3. football
4. drama
5. orchestra
6. pep squad
7. school newspaper
8. community service
9. student government

B. WHICH GROUP?

Music	Clubs	Writing
band	chess	newspaper
orchestra	debate	yearbook

WORKBOOK PAGES 119–120

A. MATCHING

1. multiplication
2. subtraction
3. division
4. addition

B. MATCHING

1. –
2. ×
3. =
4. +
5. ÷

C. LISTENING

Listen and circle the answer.

1. A. How much is three times two?
   B. Three times two equals six.
2. A. How much is four plus five?
   B. Four plus five equals nine.
3. A. How much is nine divided by three?
   B. Nine divided by three equals three.
4. A. How much is eight minus two?
   B. Eight minus two equals six.
5. A. How much is two times five?
   B. Two times five equals ten.

Answers

1. ×
2. +
3. ÷
4. –
5. ×

D. WRITE THE MATH PROBLEMS

1. $1 + 6 = 7$
2. $8 \div 4 = 2$
3. $2 \times 5 = 10$
4. $12 - 7 = 5$

E. WHAT'S THE FRACTION?

1/4 1/2 1/3 2/3 3/4

F. MATCHING

1. 1/2
2. 1/4
3. 2/3
4. 3/4
5. 1/3

G. LISTENING

Listen and circle the answer.

1. A. Is this on sale?
   B. Yes. It's one third off the regular price.
   A. One third off the regular price?
   B. That's right.
2. A. Is this on sale?
   B. Yes. It's one half off the regular price.
   A. One half off the regular price?
   B. That's right.
3. A. Is this on sale?
   B. Yes. It's one quarter off the regular price.
   A. One quarter off the regular price?
   B. That's right.
4. A. The gas tank is three quarters full.
   B. Three quarters?
   A. Yes.
5. A. The gas tank is half full.
   B. Half full?
   A. Yes.

Answers

1. 1/3
2. 1/2
3. 1/4
4. 3/4
5. 1/2

H. WHAT'S THE PERCENT?

25%   75%   50%   100%

I. MATCHING

1. 50%
2. 25%
3. 100%
4. 30%
5. 75%

J. LISTENING

Listen and write the percent you hear.

1. A. There's a fifty percent chance of rain.
   B. Fifty percent?
   A. Yes.
2. A. There's a one hundred percent chance of rain.
   B. One hundred percent?
   A. Yes.
3. A. How did you do on the test?
   B. I got ninety percent of the answers right.
   A. Ninety percent?
   B. Yes.
4. A. How did you do on the test?
   B. I got seventy-five percent of the answers right.
   A. Seventy-five percent?
   B. Yes.
5. A. Is this on sale?
   B. Yes. It's twenty-five percent off the regular price.
   A. Twenty-five percent?
   B. Yes. That's right.
6. A. Is this on sale?
   B. Yes. It's ten percent off the regular price.
   A. Ten percent?
   B. Yes. That's right.

Answers

1. 50%
2. 100%
3. 90%
4. 75%
5. 25%
6. 10%

WORKBOOK PAGES 121–122

A. WHAT'S THE WORD?

1. circle
2. square
3. line
4. triangle
5. rectangle
6. cube
7. cylinder
8. cone
9. pyramid
10. angle
11. sphere
12. ellipse

B. WHICH GROUP?

Triangle	Circle
base	diameter
hypotenuse	radius

Rectangle	
length	
width	

C. WHAT'S THE WORD?

a. inch
b. foot
c. yard
d. centimeter
e. meter

D. MATCHING: *Abbreviations*

1. centimeter
2. meter
3. mile
4. kilometer
5. inch
6. foot
7. yard

E. WHAT'S THE ANSWER?

1. 1"
2. 12"
3. 1 yd.
4. 1 mi.
5. 3'
6. 1'

WORKBOOK PAGES 123–124

A. WHAT'S THE PART OF SPEECH?

1. f
2. c
3. e
4. g
5. d
6. a
7. b

B. MATCHING: *Types of Sentences*

1. imperative
2. interrogative
3. exclamatory
4. declarative

C. MATCHING: *Parts of Speech*

1. verb
2. adjective
3. article
4. noun
5. verb
6. preposition
7. noun
8. pronoun

D. MATCHING: *Punctuation Marks*

1. period
2. comma
3. question mark
4. quotation marks
5. apostrophe
6. exclamation point
7. colon
8. semi-colon

E. FIX THE SENTENCES

1. My sister's name is Berta.
2. What's your telephone number**?**
3. These cookies are fantastic**!**
4. Please get milk**,** eggs, and bread at the supermarket.
5. My children are in elementary school**.**
6. Our school has three music activities**:** the band, the orchestra, and the choir.

F. THE WRITING PROCESS

1. ideas
2. draft
3. corrections
4. feedback
5. final

WORKBOOK PAGE 125

A. CHOOSE THE CORRECT WORD

1. biography
2. editorial
3. invitation
4. postcard
5. note
6. letter

B. MATCHING

1. thank-you note
2. autobiography
3. postcard
4. invitation
5. instant message
6. editorial

C. WHICH GROUP?

Fiction	Non-Fiction
novel	autobiography
short story	biography

Mail
letter
postcard

WORKBOOK PAGE 126

A. WHAT'S THE WORD?

a. forest
b. hill
c. lake
d. waterfall
e. river
f. rainforest

B. WHAT IS IT?

1. river
2. island
3. desert
4. lake
5. canyon
6. peninsula

C. WHICH GROUP?

Land	Water
desert	lake
meadow	ocean
mountain	pond
plains	river

WORKBOOK PAGE 127

A. WHAT'S THE WORD?

1. flask
2. scale
3. prism
4. magnet
5. beaker
6. microscope
7. dropper
8. funnel
9. test tube

B. MATCHING

1. tongs
2. dish
3. burner
4. cylinder
5. method

WORKBOOK PAGE 128

A. WHAT'S THE OCCUPATION?

1. chef
2. baker
3. assembler
4. cashier
5. carpenter
6. accountant

B. MATCHING: *Who Uses It?*

1. chef
2. carpenter
3. artist
4. cashier
5. barber

WORKBOOK PAGE 129

A. WHAT'S THE OCCUPATION?

1. custodian
2. farmer
3. firefighter
4. factory worker
5. garment worker
6. food-service worker

B. MATCHING: *Who Uses It?*

1. custodian
2. data entry clerk
3. food-service worker
4. gardener
5. hairdresser

WORKBOOK PAGE 130

A. WHAT'S THE OCCUPATION?

1. pilot
2. lawyer
3. pharmacist
4. mover
5. mechanic
6. manicurist

B. MATCHING

1. receptionist
2. mechanic
3. pharmacist
4. housekeeper
5. manicurist

WORKBOOK PAGE 131

A. WHAT'S THE OCCUPATION?

1. teacher
2. welder
3. secretary
4. waiter
5. waitress
6. translator

B. CROSSWORD

(See page 172.)

WORKBOOK PAGE 132

A. WHAT DO THEY DO?

1. cook
2. clean
3. deliver
4. file
5. drive
6. assemble

B. MATCHING

1. cook.
2. act.
3. drive.
4. mow lawns.
5. assemble components.
6. build things.
7. clean.
8. fly airplanes.

WORKBOOK PAGE 133

A. WHAT DO THEY DO?

1. paint
2. sew
3. sell
4. wash
5. type
6. serve

B. MATCHING

1. paints.
2. types.
3. serves food.
4. supervises people.
5. sells things.

WORKBOOK PAGE 134

A. CHOOSE THE CORRECT WORD

1. sign
2. classified ad
3. job notice
4. application
5. interview
6. benefits

B. MATCHING: *Abbreviations*

1. hour
2. evenings
3. full-time
4. part-time
5. previous
6. required
7. experience
8. available
9. Monday through Friday
10. excellent

WORKBOOK PAGE 135

A. CHOOSE THE CORRECT WORD

1. time clock
2. suggestion box
3. shipping clerk
4. forklift

5. conveyor belt
6. assembly line
7. loading dock
8. hand truck
9. payroll office

B. MATCHING

1. clock
2. line
3. station
4. box
5. belt

WORKBOOK PAGE 136

A. WHAT'S THE WORD?

1. crane
2. ladder
3. bulldozer
4. wire
5. backhoe
6. dump truck
7. wood
8. brick
9. wheelbarrow

B. WHICH GROUP?

Materials	Machines
beam	backhoe
pipe	bulldozer
plywood	cement mixer

WORKBOOK PAGE 137

A. WHAT'S THE WORD?

1. helmet
2. mask
3. hairnet
4. first-aid kit
5. back support
6. safety glasses

B. MATCHING

1. head
2. eyes
3. face
4. feet
5. hands

C. LISTENING: *Warnings*

Listen and write the number under the correct picture.

1. A. Don't forget to wear your safety earmuffs!
   B. Thanks for reminding me.
2. A. Be careful! That's poisonous!
   B. Thanks for the warning.
3. A. Watch out! That's flammable!
   B. Thanks for the warning.
4. A. Don't forget to wear your hard hat!
   B. Thanks for reminding me.
5. A. Be careful! That material is corrosive!
   B. Thanks for the warning.
6. A. Be careful! That work area is radioactive!
   B. Thanks for the warning.

Answers

5	3	2	6	1	4

WORKBOOK PAGE 138

A. WHAT'S THE WORD?

1. bus
2. taxi
3. bus station
4. conductor
5. ticket
6. train
7. bus driver
8. bus stop
9. ferry

B. MATCHING

1. counter
2. stop
3. card
4. compartment
5. booth

A. WHAT'S THE WORD?

1. off	5. over
2. on	6. under
3. down	7. into
4. up	8. out of

B. LISTENING: *Following Directions*

Listen and write the number under the correct picture.

1. Walk down this street.
2. Go around the corner.
3. Walk across the street.
4. Go over the bridge.
5. Drive under the bridge.
6. Go past the bank.

Answers

6	2	4
5	3	1

WORKBOOK PAGE 140

A. MATCHING: *What's the Sign?*

1. no right turn
2. no left turn
3. no U-turn
4. right turn only
5. pedestrian crossing
6. slippery when wet
7. school crossing
8. railroad crossing

B. WHAT'S THE COMPASS DIRECTION?

	north	
west		east
	south	

C. LISTENING: *Traffic Signs*

Listen and write the number under the correct sign.

1. You have to stop. There's a stop sign.
2. This is handicapped parking only.
3. Don't turn right. The sign says "no right turn".
4. Careful! That sign says "merging traffic".
5. You can't go on that street. Do you see the sign?

Answers

3	1	5	2	4

WORKBOOK PAGE 141

A. CHOOSE THE CORRECT WORD

1. ticket
2. suitcase
3. customs officer
4. passport
5. boarding pass
6. security officer
7. security checkpoint
8. baggage claim area

B. MATCHING

1. officer	4. pass
2. checkpoint	5. detector
3. counter	

WORKBOOK PAGE 142

A. WHAT'S THE WORD?

1. beach	6. aquarium
2. zoo	7. play
3. museum	8. carnival
4. concert	9. mountains
5. movies	

B. MATCHING

1. sale	4. gardens
2. market	5. park
3. gallery	

WORKBOOK PAGE 143

A. CROSSWORD

(See page 172.)

B. MATCHING

1. pong	4. skating
2. arts	5. tennis
3. riding	

WORKBOOK PAGE 144

A. WHAT'S THE SPORT?

1. basketball	4. ice hockey
2. football	5. baseball
3. soccer	6. lacrosse

B. WHICH GROUP?

Field	Rink	Court
baseball	ice hockey	basketball
soccer		volleyball

WORKBOOK PAGE 145

A. CHOOSE THE CORRECT WORD

1. jazz	4. cartoon
2. rock music	5. comedy
3. ballet	6. game show

B. LISTENING

Listen. Write the number next to the type of music you hear.

1. (Sound: popular music)
2. (Sound: classical music)
3. (Sound: country music)
4. (Sound: jazz)
5. (Sound: rock)
6. (Sound: hip hop)

Answers

2	6	1
4	5	3

(continued)

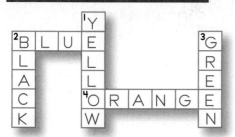

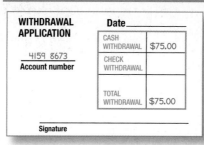

	1256
	(date) _____ 20___
Pay to the Order of City Power	$ 75.80
Seventy-five and 80/100 ─────────── Dollars	
First National Bank 1200 West 45th Street Chicago, IL 60609	
For _____	(signature)

⑈01234567⑈ 321 1 123456⑈ 0000

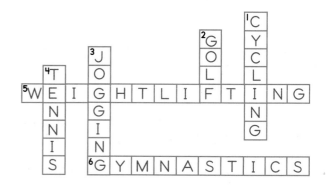